INDOOR BONSAI

Paul Lesniewicz

INDOOR BONSAI

Translated by Susan Simpson

**EVERYTHING YOU NEED TO KNOW ABOUT
INDOOR BONSAI: SELECTION, CARE & DISPLAY**

Title of the original German edition: Bonsai für die Wohnung
– Verlag Bonsai Centrum Heidelberg

First published in the UK in 1985 by Blandford Press

First published in this edition in 2004 by Cassell Illustrated,
an imprint of Octopus Publishing Group Ltd
Carmelite House
50 Victoria Embankment
London EC4Y 0DZ
www.octopusbooks.co.uk

An Hachette UK Company
www.hachette.co.uk

This edition published in 2021

Distributed in the US by Hachette Book Group
1290 Avenue of the Americas, 4th and 5th Floors
New York, NY 10020

Distributed in Canada by Canadian Manda Group
664 Annette St.
Toronto, Ontario, Canada M6S 2C8

ISBN 978-1-78840-301-6

Typeset by August Filmsetting, Haydocks, St Helens

Printed and bound in China

1 3 5 7 9 10 8 6 4 2

Acknowledgements
In putting this book together I have been helped and advised by Ilona Lesniewicz,
Leni Stockmann-Mayer, Henry Lorenz and Wolfgang Dethmers.

The following were kind enough to allow me the use of their photographs: Jyoti and Nikunj Parekh,
India; Kindai-Bonsai, Japan; Hiroshi Takeyama, Japan; Yu Yat Shan, Hong Kong, China; Chen
Ming Lun, Hong Kong, China; Huang Te Chang, Taiwan, China; Yin Chin Chang, Taiwan, China;
Marius Greeff, South Africa; Dr Gustavo Bataller, Spain; Giorgi Gianfranco, Italy;
Guido Degl' Innocenti, Italy; Umberto Margiacchi, Italy; Josef Wiegand, Germany.

Photographic material: Bonsai Centrum Heidelberg
Drawings: Willi Benz

The publishers would like to thank Peter M. Brown FRCS, Chairman of the British Federation
of Bonsai Societies, for his help and advice in the English translation of this book.

Contents

What is Bonsai?

Legend has it that in the fourth century A.D. the Chinese poet and civil servant Guen-ming, having retired from his official post, started to grow chrysanthemums in pots which he would bring into his home and place on his veranda. This may well have been the beginning of potted plant cultivation.

Some 200 years later a new art, later called bonsai, was to develop from this. Paintings from the T'ang dynasty (618-906) show pine trees, cypresses, plums, bamboos and sageretias growing in pots, and bonsai has been a feature of Chinese culture ever since, found virtually all over Asia today.

Over the centuries it was the Japanese who perfected the art of growing miniature trees to look like their larger natural counterparts, and they gave us the word bonsai — 'bon' meaning pot, and 'sai', tree. The height of a bonsai tree is usually between 20 and 70 cm (8 and 28 in).

In tropical parts of the world, such as southern China, Thailand, and Singapore, bonsai specimens

Painting dating from the T'ang dynasty showing a bonsai in the foreground.

(Opposite) Japanese woodcut: a bonsai grower offering some of his specimens for sale.

7

A tropical forest where the trees grow high into the sky. (Photo: Renate von Forster.)

are also cultivated from plants such as fig trees, carmonas (Fukien tea) and bougainvilleas, species which have long been used as houseplants to decorate homes.

Europeans, however, despite lavishing a great deal of care on their plants, never seemed to have stumbled on the idea of training them to recapture their original form. Perhaps visions of tree-high ferns and 40-m-high fig trees stopped them, for there would never be enough room for them on balconies or inside houses. Yet we know that tropical and subtropical plants do well in the indoor climate, perhaps not growing 'high into the sky', but rather developing miniature forms.

When shaping their bonsai, Asiatic peoples follow Zen Buddhist principles, the aim being to create something natural, simple and asymmetrical while concentrating on what is most essential. Disciples of Zen Buddhism seek harmony between man and nature, and regard bonsai trees as religious objects which help in meditation.

For a European interested in bonsai this religious background and meditative tradition is something alien, but he can learn nevertheless to set aside time just to look at his miniature trees, and to enjoy the sense of creativity as he determines their shape, making them grow more and more like natural trees in every respect except size.

Creating and looking after a bonsai involves a

certain degree of skill, but anyone who has had some success with plants in general will quickly learn the art and derive great pleasure from it.

Indoor bonsai adapted for the West

In America and Europe it was people living in big cities who were among the first to discover bonsai as a hobby. Having a real tree – the symbol of all life – meant more than bedecking one's home with greenery, making it more attractive and alive with plants. It was a new approach to nature, long before nature had become fashionable again.

In temperate latitudes people live indoors more than out. More often than not, in order to admire the beauty of traditional bonsai one has to look out through the window, as the collection is usually found out on the balcony or veranda. This book sets out to describe how to create and care for bonsai that can be brought indoors.

Indoor bonsai are miniature versions of subtropical and tropical trees and shrubs, whose native climate corresponds most closely with the climate inside the house. Many of the species of plant used have already had a place inside as pot plants for decades.

Indoor bonsai are not ordinary pot plants

Plants with small leaves and branches that are not too woody are particularly good for training as bonsai. To achieve a harmonious effect of branches, leaves, flowers and fruits that are all in proportion, species with delicate flowers and small fruits are preferred. Miniature trees are not shaped by genetic changes, so the bonsai grower has little influence upon the size of flowers and fruits; he can only make branches and leaves smaller. For this reason mini mandarin trees with their fingernail-sized fruits are more suitable for training than orange trees.

For trees and shrubs that flourish in a temperate climate the differences between summer and winter, and day and night, are of vital importance. In the constant temperatures of Western homes they would only survive for a short while. Many tropical plants

The origins of indoor bonsai

An old olive tree – the 'big brother' of many a delightful indoor specimen. (Photo: Josef Wiegand.)

are suited to this indoor climate because in their native countries there are scarcely any seasons and little variation in temperature. Vegetation there grows almost non-stop, unlike the dormancy of European and North American trees during winter. Particularly in the tropical rain forests where it is always warm and damp, an enormous profusion of magnificent trees and plants can thrive, often living for hundreds of years. It is here that can be found full-grown models for some very attractive indoor bonsai: fig trees, bamboos, scheffleras and jacarandas, to name but a few. Azaleas, citrus trees, camellias, pomegranates, myrtles, olive trees and many other lovely and interesting plants originate from the Mediterranean area, in other words from subtropical regions. These can be grown as bonsai for indoors and out.

Optimum conditions for Indoor Bonsai

Always remember that a house does not entirely correspond to the natural environment of the miniature trees, even if they are doing well indoors. Like that of a human, the life of a plant is made up of a never-ending cycle of events that are influenced by light, air, temperature, humidity, day and night, summer and winter. To grow indoor bonsai successfully and gain satisfaction from them it is advisable to know a little about their origin and the life cycle of their 'big brothers' in nature.

Temperature

Plant species from tropical and subtropical climatic zones are classified by horticulturists according to their warmth requirements. Tropical plants must be kept in 'hot-houses' with a temperature of at least 18–24°C (64–75°F), because they are accustomed to fairly constant temperatures throughout the year. You should allow the temperature to drop at night by 2–4°C (4–8°F), but never let it fall below 16°C (60°F). Your fig tree, schefflera or Ming aralia can therefore safely be placed at a window directly above a radiator. At night, again make sure that the temperature does not fall below the lowest recommended level. Also take special care if you have thick curtains, as they keep out warmth from inside the room and retain the cold from outside in the window area.

Subtropical species need 'cold-houses' with a winter temperature of 5–12°C (41–54°F). They undergo a dormant period during the cold season and so cannot tolerate too high temperatures. During this time they should be placed in a cool, bright room – a bedroom, hallway or conservatory. In the homelands of species such as citrus trees, camellias and azaleas, the winter temperature does not climb above 15°C (59°F), nor dip below 5–6°C (41–43°F) at night. So, for subtropical bonsai, the aim should be to create a climate as near to this as possible.

To lower the temperature at night simply move the trees to a cooler site, or create a cooler 'climatic zone' around the window area by means of a heavy curtain. Cold-house bonsai should not be placed directly over a radiator, although many cold-house species are able to adapt to a warmer climate and tolerate a surrounding temperature of a few degrees higher. In such cases the trees do not necessarily become completely dormant during winter; their growth simply slows up. Deciduous species will retain some of their leaves, whereas in a cooler site they would lose them all.

Even if you have placed your cold-house bonsai in a warmer location do not forget to lower the night temperature. In most houses this is not a problem as the heating is already turned down at night as an economy measure.

In summer, although not imperative, it is of benefit to place cold-house bonsai outside, provided that they are sheltered from the wind. Initially, it is important to provide some shade, so that the plant can gradually become accustomed to air and sun – about two weeks in all. Bring the trees inside again in autumn, no later than when the night temperature outside drops to 6°C (43°F).

(Opposite) Free-standing trees like this stone-pine make the best models for bonsai shaping. (Photo: Tell Leeser.)

Sufficient light is of vital importance to your indoor bonsai, for without it the plant cannot live, as light is needed for the essential process of photosynthesis. The ideal position is invariably near a bright window. Just 1 m (3 ft) away from the window the light intensity is considerably reduced, enough to make it too dark for many plants, although the difference is scarcely detectable with the human eye. Even a translucent curtain significantly reduces the light intensity. Nearly every window is bright enough, provided that it is not too overshadowed by the roof, by trees or neighbouring houses.

Light does not mean hot sunshine, but brightness. Too much heat can be harmful to your plants, and even kill them. That is why in the very hot summer months any bonsai at a south- or west-facing window must be protected from the strongest rays of the sun by a blind or curtain. A newspaper placed between plant and window also affords good protection from the sun.

Light intensity is measured with a light meter; this is a simple instrument, similar to a photographer's exposure meter. The unit of measure is known as a lux; an indoor bonsai requires a minimum of 200–1,000 lux during the day, and some species need more than this (see page 16). If your bonsai is receiving too little light, boost the amount with artificial light. Leave any supplementary lighting switched on for at least 6–8 hours during the day.

With the right lighting indoor bonsai will even thrive in a 'dark' corner of the room – provided that the temperature and humidity levels are suitable.

Whenever artificial light is used almost exclusively for indoor bonsai, the lights must be burned for 10–16 hours, depending on their light intensity. An automatic timing device is not expensive and is to be highly recommended, since it is important to illuminate your plants regularly at the same time each day – holidays and weekends included.

This bonsai enthusiast keeps his collection in the kitchen. Artificial lighting is suspended from cupboards above.

Overleaf there is a list of indoor plants with their minimum light requirements denoted by a circle in the corresponding column.

The amount of light required by indoor bonsai

Whenever a circle appears in two columns in the table it means that the plant will also survive with less light, although it will grow more vigorously and have a stronger leaf and flower colour if placed somewhere brighter.

If a circle appears in the first column it denotes that the plant is particularly sensitive to the full glare of the sun. Precautionary measures should be taken in all these cases, or a window away from the direct rays of the sun should be selected.

Normal light bulbs are not suitable for illuminating plants because their light is not the same as daylight and they may cause burn damage to your plants. Special lighting filaments and tubes have been developed to provide the right frequency spectrum for photosynthesis. These include halogen quartz and iodine quartz bulbs and fluorescent tubes, including a mini version. For shelving units triple banks of lamps with three different colours of light are preferable. Fluorescent tubes, as used by aquarium keepers to provide enough light for their water plants and fish, are another possibility. Depending on the type of light source used it should be placed between 25 and 80 cm (10–30 in) above the plants. A coat of white enamel paint on the

board to which the lamps are to be attached will cut
down the need for reflectors.

Amount of light required by indoor bonsai

Plants	Sun-light	up to 200 lux	200 lux	500 lux	1000 lux
Aralia				○	
Araucaria	○			○	
Adenium				○	
Azalea				○	
Camellia	○			○	
Cissus		○		○	
Citrus				○	
Codiaenum				○	
Crassula				○	○
Cycas revoluta				○	
Dracaena					○
Echeveria					○
Eurya	○			○	
Fatshedera				○	
Ficus				○	○
Fuchsia				○	
Hedera		○		○	
Helexine				○	○
Hibiscus					○
Jacobinia				○	
Kalanchoe					○
Nerium				○	
Nolina					○
Olea				○	○
Ophiopogon				○	
Pelargonium					○
Pereskia				○	
Pilea				○	
Poinsettia				○	
Portulacaria afra					○
Punica				○	
Rhododendron simsii				○	
Rosmarinum				○	○
Saxifraga				○	
Schefflera				○	○
Selaginella				○	
Solanum				○	
Sparmannia	○			○	○
Spurge				○	
Succulents				○	○

Glass shelving unit for housing a large bonsai collection. One light source is enough for quite a number of indoor specimens.

As your bonsai collection becomes bigger, you will not always have access to the best site at just the right window. Some glass shelving may solve the problems and provide the right light for your bonsai, as well as being decorative and economical. One source of artificial light will be enough to supply all the plants on the shelving unit – a rotating iodine-quartz lamp, for example, produces about 2000 lux from a distance of 80 cm (30 in). The light intensity decreases the further away the light source is, so plants that need plenty of light should be placed nearer the lamp.

The best way to arrange your collection

Sufficient humidity is vital for every indoor bonsai, for when the air is dry the plant 'transpires', i.e. it loses more water through evaporation than it takes in via the roots. The stomata on the underside of the leaf close up, gas exchange is interrupted and growth is therefore impeded.

It is easy to understand, therefore, why a hygrometer is such an indispensable tool to every indoor gardener. It is an instrument for measuring relative humidity, or the ratio of the amount of water vapour in the air to the amount that would saturate it at the same temperature. The warmer the room, the greater the amount of water vapour required to maintain the same degree of relative humidity.

You can judge how resilient your bonsai are to air that is too dry by looking at them. Shiny, leathery leaves – as found in fig trees, for example – point to a small amount of water loss through evaporation. Such plants are less endangered than bonsai with large, soft or herbaceous leaves which lose a great deal of water through evaporation (e.g. *Lantana, Punica*).

Tray filled with gravel to increase humidity.

The humidity level of living-rooms conducive to indoor bonsai should register at least 40–50 per cent. Compared to our dry, overheated homes in winter, this would be a better level for humans and animals alike, not to mention the furniture (in museums they always install humidifiers). Even if you decide not to install electric humidifiers, at least take steps to create a higher humidity in the immediate vicinity of the plants. Either place water-filled dishes or a room fountain near the bonsai, or use the old trick of hanging water-filled containers over the central heating radiators. Another solution is to stand your bonsai, complete with dish, on a tray filled with a layer of pebbles that are kept permanently moist.

Water-filled dishes and containers are also important for taking care of your plants while you are away on holiday (see p. 27).

The plants will benefit from a regular spraying, as well as watering, as this temporarily increases the humidity level.

It is also a good idea to give bonsai trees a luke-warm shower in the bath every four weeks to get rid of any dust. This will enable the plants to breathe properly again, something they cannot do if dust particles are clogging up the stomata.

Fresh air is also important for plants. In summer this presents no problem, but in winter when you open any window make sure that your tropical trees are not caught in a draught, and above all that it is not frosty.

A bonsai window display.

Important points regarding siting of bonsai

Temperature	Tropical bonsai require a winter temperature throughout the day of between 18°C and 24°C (64–75°F). At night they can tolerate a temperature reduction of around 2–4°C (4–8°F). Subtropical bonsai prefer a cooler winter temperature, the ideal being 10–15°C (50–59°F) by day and 6–10°C (43–50°F) by night. However, they can also 'overwinter' at somewhat warmer temperatures. In summer cold-house bonsai can also be placed out-of-doors, but remember they will need time to adapt to the new conditions.
Light	You will need a light meter. 1) Your choice of site for your bonsai will depend on the light requirements of the plant (see table on p. 16). 2) If the natural light is insufficient, supplement with artificial light. 3) Too strong sunlight is dangerous for your plants. 4) Too little light makes the shoots longer and more spindly.
Air	You will need a hygrometer. Bonsai trees with large, soft leaves are particularly susceptible to dry, centrally-heated air. The humidity level in the vicinity of your plants should be at least 40–50 per cent. In winter it is a good idea to make use of electric humidifiers or water-filled containers in centrally-heated homes.

(Opposite) Bonsai window display with, from left to right, Sageretia, Euphorbia, Sedum, Nandina.

Constant Care

The most important points regarding temperature, light and air were covered in the previous section. This part shows how to care for your bonsai, including watering and feeding them, and looking after them when you are on holiday.

Watering

Correct watering is absolutely essential if your indoor bonsai is to remain healthy. Remember however, that what is correct for one plant is not necessarily right for another. An azalea, for example, needs much more water than a cactus.

One thing is true for all indoor bonsai: they need water before the soil has become completely dry. You can often tell how much moisture there is in the soil from its colour – the paler the earth, the drier it is. If you are not sure from looking at it, you can also try the 'tapping test' to see if your plant needs watering. Tap the pot on a table or bench; if it sounds hollow, the soil must have already come away from the side of the pot, so it is high time for the plant to be watered.

Always water onto the soil, slowly, and pausing briefly to allow the soil to soak up all it wants. Keep watering until water starts to flow from the drainage holes. Then stop. It should be noted that if the soil is very dry water cannot be absorbed instantly. It will flow straight out through the drainage holes. In this case immerse the tree in water (see page 98).

Avoid spraying plants out in the sun. Drops of water on the leaves can focus the sun's rays and cause burns. If you feel it necessary to top up your bonsai with water in the middle of a hot summer's day because the plant is all 'limp', only water its soil or take the plant out of the sun. Bonsai should not be sprayed in the evening either, because if there is not enough time for the plant to dry off before the onset of night fungi and bacteria may attack it.

Bonsai in very small pots may also be immersed in water, instead of watering in the normal way. Stand the plant in enough water to let it come up over the edge of the pot and leave it there until you can see no more air bubbles (this takes around five minutes). This shows that the soil is fully saturated with water. The immersion technique is also suitable if ever the soil has become powder-dry and the leaves of your tree are hanging limply.

Novice bonsai growers can experience disappointing results with their plants because they have been over- or underwatered. In winter, for example, it is easy to overwater, particularly cold-house plants which grow more slowly at this time of year and so need less water. Bonsai positioned directly above a radiator can just as easily be underwatered, because a plant in such a site demands a lot of water.

The water you use should be soft, i.e. it should contain as little calcium as possible and have no more than 12–15 degrees of hardness. Very hard water can after a time effect a chemical change in the soil; the pH value will rise, and its degree of acidity will therefore decrease. The ideal is 8–9 degrees of hardness, a level which will ensure that the pH value is also correct: 5.5–6.5. You can find out the degree of hardness of your tap water by asking the appropriate water authority or by talking to a local horticulturist. If your water is too hard, you will soon know when off-white chalky deposits collect around the trunk of your tree and around the inner edge of your pot. If this happens, you can soften the water either by boiling it or by using a biological softening agent but it is more satisfactory to use a commercial iron exchange resin or even rainwater.

Never use completely cold water for your bonsai – it should be as near room temperature as possible. Simply let the water stand for a while before use in the watering can. Water that is cold makes the soil cold too, and this prevents the plant from absorbing water and nutrients.

If the soil remains moist for a long time without being watered, there is something wrong with the plant's mechanism for absorbing water and the root system may be damaged.

Unlike its larger counterpart in nature, the indoor bonsai has only a very limited amount of soil from which to obtain its food. That is why it is very important to keep replenishing the soil with nutrients.

What to Feed

For a plant the most important minerals are nitrogen, phosphorus, potash, calcium, sulphur, iron and various trace elements. The plant can be provided with these either in the form of salts (i.e. purely inorganic fertilisers), or in the form of organic fertilisers, such as bonemeal, horn, blood etc.

Mineralised organic fertilisers in powder form that are sprinkled on the surface of the soil have received good reports. They are a mixture of short- and long-term fertilisers. The mineral components dissolve in water, and are then instantly absorbed by the roots and used up quickly. The organic components go to work more gradually and so have a more long-term effect.

Do not use the same feed all the time during the growing season. Alternate between powder and liquid versions.

Pellets are one form of fertiliser disliked by the indoor gardener. Although popular with keepers of outdoor bonsai, they do spread an unpleasant smell in the confines of a room.

(Opposite) **Murraya paniculata,** *approximately 80 years old and 75 cm (30 in) high.*

How is feed added?   Provided you stick to the most important rules, there
should be no problems with feeding your bonsai.

1) Water thoroughly before adding feed.

2) It is better to add a little fertiliser more often than
to add too much infrequently.

3) With liquid feeds use the amounts given in the
instructions for potted plants. If anything, use a bit
less than it says; never more.

4) Powdered organic feeds should be sprinkled
evenly on to the surface of the soil.

5) You cannot make a mistake with feeds made
specifically for bonsai.

If your bonsai looks dull and wretched, it may be a
sign that you have used too much feed rather than
too little. Often it means that the root area is
damaged, something which may not always be
caused by too much fertiliser, but which precludes
any further feeding in any case. Another sign that
your roots may be unhealthy is when the plant uses
much less water than usual. In this case remove the
tree from its pot and inspect the roots. If they are
white and firm, the tree is healthy. If the tips of the
roots look brown and mushy and can easily be
pulled out, they are dead and can no longer absorb
food. Snip the dead roots off and plant the bonsai in
some fresh earth. Only begin to feed again once the
tree has acquired new roots.

Not all bonsai need the same amount of nutrients. The requirements for different plants are given on pp. 32–86. As a general rule young and growing trees need fertiliser more often than old ones. Fast-growing species must be fed more often than slow-growing ones.

When to add fertiliser

Most tropical bonsai will grow all year round indoors, more quickly between spring and autumn, and significantly more slowly in winter. So they should be fed more frequently in the main growing season and less often in the winter months. Subtropical (cold-house) bonsai, located in a cool site, become dormant in winter and so do not require additional nutrients.

1) Shortly before and during the flowering period. The increased vigour would go into the shoots, and the tree would shed its buds and flowers. Once fruits have formed, resume feeding.
2) After repotting and root pruning (see pp. 93–99). the root system has to regenerate. Suspend feeding for about four to six weeks.
3) During winter dormancy.
4) Plants with damaged roots cannot absorb fertiliser, so feeding must cease in this case too.

When not to add fertiliser

When holidays loom, experienced indoor gardeners will only entrust their bonsai to a system of care that they have tried out beforehand. It is advisable to test the method you have selected while you are still at home. Of course it all depends on how long you will be away. If you are one of those lucky people who can take three or four weeks' holiday, please ask friends or neighbours to check through your care plan a couple of times and, if necessary, correct it. Inexperienced 'bonsai sitters' need to be told that too much water can be just as damaging as too little. Many people water too much from fear that the bonsai might die of thirst.

Care in the holiday period

The tips given below have all been tried out by keepers of indoor bonsai. Common to them all is that they will work better if the bonsai is placed in not too warm a spot and out of the sun.

Short holidays, up to six days

Your bonsai will easily last out such a short period. Simply water thoroughly, then sink the pot into a box or plastic bowl filled with very damp peat.

Another suggestion involves constructing an enclosed system for the plants from which water cannot escape through evaporation but is retained inside. Firstly water your bonsai thoroughly, then stand them inside a large, transparent plastic bag

Plastic trough containing moist peat – a simple device for looking after bonsai when you are away on a short holiday.

punched with a few holes, and tied at the top. To allow the plant sufficient room and to stop the bag falling onto it as condensation builds up, make a form of support using some thin wire. Hardly any water will be able to escape from this micro-environment you have created, and the plant will remain moist. Make sure you remove any half-withered flowers and yellowing leaves before placing in the bag, as they may fall off and cause rotting.

A 'mini greenhouse' made out of a plastic bag supported by wire.

There are basically three types of watering system which can be effectively employed if you are to be away from home for a longer period of time. These are capillary matting, drip irrigation and gravel trays. All of these systems are commercially produced and available from garden centres, who will be able to give you advice on which type to use for your particular plants and circumstances.

If you are away from home during winter, make sure that your heating is not turned off completely and that temperatures of 16–18°C (61–64°F) are maintained for your tropical bonsai.

Holidays lasting up to two or more weeks

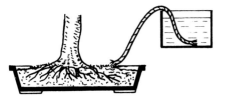

A piece of wool links a bonsai to a water supply placed on a higher level.

Important points regarding constant care

Watering	Never allow the soil to dry out completely.
	Do not spray a plant out in the sun or pour water onto the leaves.
	Boil very hard tap water or use a softening agent.
	Always use water at room temperature.
	If your bonsai does not use any water, check its roots.
Feeding	Always water first before feeding.
	It is better to use too little than too much fertiliser, particularly if you are using a mineralised, i.e. inorganic, feed.
	Young and fast-growing trees need more feeding than old and slow-growing species.
	Do not use the same fertilisers all through the growing season; alternate instead.
	Do not feed your plants shortly before and during the flowering period, after repotting, after root pruning, during the dormant period and when the tree is unhealthy.

(Opposite)
Podocarpus
macrophyllus,
*approximately 95
years old and 75 cm
(30 in) high. From
the collection of Yee-
sun Wu, Hong Kong.*

Indoor Bonsai Species

On the following pages you will find everything you need to know about training and caring for all the most popular indoor bonsai species. The information given applies to the plants named in the headings as well as the majority of the other plants belonging to the same family. For example, you can use the instructions given for *Buxus harlandii* with all box tree species.

Buxus harlandii, *approximately 70 years old and 65 cm (25 in) high. From the collection of Te Chang Huang, Taiwan.*

Family: Buxaceae
Native to: Japan, Eastern Asia, Mediterranean area

Buxus harlandii
Box tree

A richly-branching, robust, evergreen ornamental shrub with small, shiny, dark green, leathery leaves. Grows slowly. Trained into regular, geometric shapes in baroque gardens or used as a garden border, although it is more familiar as a thick hedge. Has long been trained as a bonsai in Taiwan.

Site All year round at a bright, cool, north-, east-, or west-facing window, never a south-facing one. May also be placed outside in semi-shade from the end of spring until early autumn. Ideal winter temperature 10–15°C (50–59°F), but can tolerate up to 20°C (68°F).

Watering During the summer water thoroughly, allow to become fairly dry; then water thoroughly again. During the winter the amount of watering will depend on the site; in a cool spot water sparingly, in a warm one water more or less as summer.

Feeding Every three weeks from spring to autumn using a liquid feed. Stop feeding in winter if plant is in a cool spot; if in a warmer position feed every six weeks.

Repotting Every two years in the spring, along with root pruning.

Soil Loam, peat and sand mixture (2:1:2).

Pruning Branches may be pruned at any time. Prune new shoots back to two or three leaf pairs once six have developed.

Wiring At any time during the year.

Propagation Cuttings.

Camellia japonica, *approximately 100 years old and 83 cm (33 in) high. From the collection of Hiroshi Takeyama, Japan.*

Family: Theaceae
Native to: Japan, China

In its native subtropical homeland and in many Mediterranean gardens the camellia grows as a richly flowering tree, 3–8 m (10–26 ft) high. It has a light silver, woody trunk and shiny, dark green, leathery leaves. Flowers appear from early winter to early spring, the colours of which may be white, pink or red. Camellias are familiar as pot plants which can be bought in almost any flower shop. They make very attractive bonsai, their compact, upright growth making them suitable for all bonsai styles. The plant will retain its capacity to bloom, provided that it is not kept too warm and is not subjected to great fluctuations in temperature.

Site A cool, airy position all year round; in summer it may be placed outside in semi-shade from late spring to early autumn, or can be kept indoors at a fairly cool, bright window facing east or north. Winter temperature 10–15°C (50–59°F); the cooler the better.

Watering Use softened water. Keep evenly moist throughout the summer. Water more sparingly in winter, but do not allow to dry out.

Feeding During the main growing season (after flowering) feed every fortnight with a liquid bonsai food or an organic plant food. Do not feed in winter.

Repotting Every two to four years in spring or after flowering. Prune roots lightly at the same time.

Soil Loam, peat and sand mixture (1:3:2).

Pruning Branches may be pruned at any time. In younger plants, in order to encourage a greater spread of branches, the new shoots should be pruned back repeatedly to two or three leaves, once four or five have formed. With older plants that already have a nice bonsai shape, prune hard only after the flowering period.

Wiring Branches at any time, shoots only from late summer once they have become mature and slightly woody. Do not apply wire to flower shoots.

Propagation Cuttings – but difficult.

Camellia japonica
Camellia

Carmona microphylla, *syn.* Erethia buxifolia, *approximately 75 years old and 68 cm (27 in) high.*

Family: Boraginaceae
Native to: Southern China, South-east Asia

A tropical, evergreen, tree-like shrub with small, oval, dark-green, shiny leaves. White flowers from spring to summer. *Carmona microphylla* forms small, green berries after blossoming, the berries gradually turning a reddish colour and tasting bitter. Highly suitable as an indoor bonsai, as it can tolerate winter temperatures of up to 24°C (75°F) in the home.

Site Indoors throughout the year at a temperature of 15–24°C (59–75°F) in a bright location, such as a west- or south-facing window. Do not allow it to bake in the sun, however; provide some shade. In summer it may also be kept outside, semi-shaded.

Carmona microphylla
Erethia buxifolia
Fukien-tea

Watering Give plenty throughout the year.

Feeding From early spring to early autumn. Feed during the main growing period every fortnight with a liquid bonsai or plant food. In winter feed about every four to six weeks.

Repotting Every two years, along with root pruning.

Soil Loam, peat, sand mixture (2:2:1).

Pruning Branches at any time. Prune new shoots back to two or three leaves once six to eight leaves have formed.

Wiring Usually *Carmona microphylla* produces an acceptable shape without wiring. Although wiring may be carried out throughout the year. Wire new shoots only once they are mature (slightly woody).

Propagation Seeds and cuttings.

Cissus antarctica, *approximately 8 years old and 25 cm (10 in) high.*

Family: Vitaceae
Native to: Australia

A nicely-branching, evergreen, climbing shrub with light-green, shiny, serrated leaves. Fast-growing. A very robust plant that can tolerate temperature variations, so it is equally well suited to a warm or cooler site.

Site Indoors throughout the year at a temperature of 15–18°C (59–64°F). A bright or more shady location is equally suitable, by an east-, west- or north-facing window, but not a south-facing one (too bright).

Watering Moderately in summer, sparingly in winter, but how sparingly will depend on whether the plant is situated in a cooler or warmer spot. Avoid getting the plant too wet around the roots, otherwise the leaves may fall off and yellowy flecks may appear.

Feeding Once a week from spring to autumn during the main growing period, using a liquid bonsai or houseplant food. Every six weeks during winter.

Repotting Young plants annually, older ones every two years in spring along with root pruning.

Soil Permeable, humus-rich loamy soil (loam, sand and peat mixture; 1:1:1).

Pruning Once four to six leaves have formed cut new growth back to two or three leaves. Leaf pruning also possible. During the main growing season keep removing any leaves that have got too big.

Wiring Possible with branches throughout the year.

Propagation Cuttings.

Cissus antarctica
Australian or
Kangaroo Vine,
Wild Grape

Crassula arborescens, *approximately 10 years old and 50 cm (20 in) high. From the collection of Maria-Luise Rieger, Germany.*

Family: Crassulaceae
Native to: South Africa

In its homeland this plant grows 2–3 m (6–10 ft) tall in a tree-like shape. Its leaves are a shiny green colour and fleshy. Highly suitable for bonsai training as it grows naturally like a tree and is often improved by shoot pruning and by thinning out its lower regions. Jade trees originate from the dry lands of South Africa and are robust, undemanding plants, if rather unusual to look at.

Site Either indoors throughout the year at a bright window, facing in any direction, or outside from late spring to early autumn in a semi-shaded spot. Winter temperature of 8–16°C (46–60°F).

Watering Moderate in summer; keep dry in winter. In summer and winter alike it can survive for four weeks at a time without water. The cooler the site, the less water needed.

Feeding Every four weeks from late spring to early autumn using a liquid bonsai or house-plant food. Do not feed in winter.

Repotting Possible at any time, but best in spring. Only trim roots slightly and do not water for fourteen days afterwards.

Soil Loam, peat and sand mixture (1:2:2).

Pruning Branches between spring and autumn. To highlight its tree-like appearance, break off the lower leaves growing on older branches (darker in colour). Once new shoots have reached the required length, nip out the tips of the shoots, leaving two to three leaf pairs.

Wiring Possible, but unnecessary.

Propagation Use cuttings 5–15 cm (2–6 in) long. Having taken your cutting, leave it to dry for about a fortnight, then stick into some dry earth (peat, sand mixture; 50:50). As soon as small white roots have developed, water thoroughly and keep moist.

Euphorbia
balsamifera,
*approximately 8
years old and 18 cm
(7 in) high.*

Family: Euphorbiaceae
Native to: Canary Islands, West Africa

This is a large family of plants with a wide variety of
growth patterns, ranging from substantial trees to
bushes and herbs, as well as cacti-like succulents.
Most species are characterised by having milk tubes.
The delicate *Euphorbia* grows like a tree and so is a
good candidate for bonsai training. Its natural shape
is often improved by the removal of unwanted
branches and the pruning of shoots.

Site Either indoors throughout the year at a bright window facing in any compass direction, or outside from late spring in a semi-shaded or sunny position. Winter temperature of 8–16°C (46–60°F) required.

Watering Moderately, about once a week, reducing to once a fortnight between mid-autumn and early spring. Should the plant lose all its leaves, cease watering until new shoots form.

Feeding Every four weeks between late spring and early autumn using a liquid bonsai or houseplant food. Do not feed during winter.

Repotting Possible at any time, but best in spring. Roots should only be trimmed slightly. Do not water for fourteen days after repotting.

Soil Loam, peat and sand mixture (1:2:2).

Pruning Branches from mid-spring to early autumn. As you are doing it, a milky substance will start to flow and run down the trunk; wash it off quickly with luke-warm water before it goes sticky. Any shoots that have grown too long can also be pruned at any time.

Wiring Possible, but not very effective.

Propagation Cuttings and seeds.

Euphorbia balsamifera
Wolfsmilk

Ficus microcarpa, *approximately 50 years old and 65 cm (25 in) high.*

Family: Moraceae
Native to: Southern and Eastern Asia

These are the legendary banyan trees of tropical Asia – enormous, shady trees with long aerial roots hanging down. All the small-leaved fig-tree species, such as *Ficus benjamina, F. retusa, F. neriifolia reg, F. benghalensis, F. religiosa* and *F. buxifola*, are good subjects for bonsai training, as they have fine strong trunks, a nice spread of branches, and shiny, evergreen, leathery leaves. Many varieties are available as pot plants that can be moulded into bonsai, but they can also be obtained quite easily from cuttings and air-layering techniques.

Site Throughout the year at a bright window facing east, west or south, but do not stand this plant in the full glare of the sun. Avoid draughts and fluctuations in temperature. Winter temperature of 18–20°C (64–68°F) required. Likes a warm soil, so avoid cold in the root area.

Watering Give plenty during the growing season from spring to autumn, but use less if sited somewhere cooler. Water sparingly in winter, allowing to dry out slightly before watering.

Feeding Every fortnight from spring to autumn using a liquid bonsai or houseplant food; about every four weeks during winter.

Repotting Every two years, ideally in spring, along with root pruning.

Soil Loam, peat and sand mixture (1:2:2).

Pruning Branches at any time. A milky fluid will flow from the wounds for a little while. Keep pruning new growth back to one to three leaves. In the main growing season leaves may also be pruned, or you may prefer simply to keep removing the largest leaves.

Wiring Possible at all times. Only woody branches should have wires attached and the wire must be removed at the right time.

Propagation Very easy using cuttings or air-layering techniques.

Ficus carica, *approximately 9 years old and 35 cm (14 in) high. From the collection of Dr Gustavo Bataller, Spain.*

Family: Moraceae
Native to: Southern Europe, North Africa

The fig tree can grow up to 6 m (20 ft) tall in its subtropical homeland. It sheds its lovely lobed leaves in the autumn. As a bonsai, it makes a charming specimen, and also forms fruits.

Site Outside in summer in a sunny position out of the wind, or inside at a warm window site. From mid-autumn cold-house conditions must be imposed, so that the tree undergoes its dormant period; therefore, stand in a cool, bright spot where the temperature is maintained around 5–8°C (41–46°F).

Watering Give plenty during the growth period from spring to autumn, but sparingly in winter during dormancy. Avoid wetness round the roots, but never allow to dry out.

Feeding Use generous amounts of liquid bonsai or houseplant food every fortnight from the time the first shoots appear in spring through till autumn.

Repotting Younger plants every two years, older ones every three to four years. Carry out along with root pruning in spring before new shoots appear.

Soil Loam, peat and sand mixture (1:1:1).

Pruning Prune back new shoots to around three leaves once six to eight have formed. During summer keep snipping out the largest leaves. A milky fluid will ooze out when pruning.

Wiring Branches throughout the year; shoots only once they have become slightly woody.

Propagation Cuttings and air-layering techniques.

Ficus carica
Fig tree

Fortunella hindsii,
*approximately 67
years old and 45 cm
(18 in) high.*

Family: Rutaceae
Native to: East Asia, Mediterranean region

Fortunella is a member of the citrus family. All the
species are subtropical, evergreen trees or shrubs,
and those that have small leaves and fruits are well
suited to bonsai training. You can either buy citrus
plants from a shop and train them as bonsai or grow
them yourself from the fruit pips. Young seedlings
will not flower very much, or will only do so 'with
age', but even without flowers dwarf orange trees
make very attractive bonsai.

Site Either outside in summer in a sunny or semi-shaded position, or inside by an airy window facing east, west or south. In winter keep cool to encourage dormancy, ideally around 6°C (43°F), and never above 12°C (54°F), otherwise some foliage will drop off.

Watering Plenty in summer; very sparingly in winter, almost letting it become dry.

Feeding Every fortnight between late spring and early autumn using a liquid bonsai or houseplant food. Suspend feeding during winter.

Repotting Every two to three years in spring before new shoots appear, at the same time as root pruning. Do not press down too deeply in the new pot. The top end of the roots must be kept free of the soil.

Soil Indoor bonsai earth or a loam, peat and sand mixture (1:1:1).

Pruning Branches at any time, but do not prune too hard, otherwise they will grow new shoots too vigorously. Seal the wounds with grafting wax. Trim back the tips of the new shoots while still soft, when around six leaves have formed. Do not prune the leaves, but keep removing any that have grown too big.

Wiring Branches throughout the year, but shoots only once they have turned slightly woody.

Propagation Seeds.

Fortunella hindsii
Dwarf orange

Gardenia
jasminoides,
*approximately 25
years old and 65 cm
(25 in) high.*

Family: Rubiaceae
Native to: China, East Asia

A richly-branching, evergreen shrub with shiny, oval-shaped, dark green, leathery leaves. Also has white, dish-shaped flowers which have a strong scent. The gardenia is familiar as a winter-flowering pot plant.

Site Inside all year round at an airy and very bright window facing north, east or west (a southerly window is too hot in summer). Ideal winter temperatures lie between 12 and 15°C (54–59°F), although if the plant is in a very warm location temperatures up to 20°C (68°F) can be tolerated.

Watering Use softened water. Water moderately in summer, less in winter, but do not allow to dry out.

Feeding Every fortnight between early spring and early autumn using a liquid bonsai or houseplant food. Do not feed in winter. If the leaves turn yellow, it is a sign of a lack of nitrogen, so some high nitrogen feed should be added.

Repotting Every one to two years in spring, along with root pruning. Requires a layer of drainage pebbles to prevent a build-up of stale water.

Soil A mixture of loam, peat and sand (1:3:2).

Wiring Branches at any time; shoots only once they have turned slightly woody. Gardenias can also be trained without wires.

Pruning Branches at any time. In older trees new shoots should be pruned hard once the flowering period is over. In younger specimens keep cutting new growth back to two to three leaves once four to six have formed.

Propagation Cuttings, but soil must be sufficiently warm (24–26°C; 75–79°F) for rooting.

Grevillea robusta,
*approximately 2
years old and 25 cm
(10 in) high.*

Family: Protaceae
Native to: Western Australia

These are the sacred trees of the Australian aborigines – truly lovely, giant species. In temperate climate they do not grow so tall, but indoor gardeners like them for their pretty, fern-like foliage and for the fact that they take little looking after.

Site Throughout the year at a bright window facing north, east or west, although *Grevillea* does not like hot sun. A winter temperature of 12–16°C (54–61°F) is required.

Watering Keep evenly moist at all times, not too wet and not too dry.

Feeding Every fortnight during the main growing season (mid-spring to early autumn) using a liquid bonsai or houseplant food. Do not feed during winter.

Repotting Annually in spring along with root pruning.

Soil Loam, peat and sand mixture (2:1:2).

Pruning Branches possible at any time. New shoots should be continually pruned back to one or two leaves. During the growing period keep removing any leaves that have grown too big.

Wiring Branches at any time. New shoots must be allowed to mature first, i.e. become slightly woody.

Propagation Cuttings and seeds.

Fuchsia fulgens
hybrida,
*approximately 6
years old and 26 cm
(10 in) high. From
the collection of
Henry Lorenz,
Germany.*

Family: Onagraceae
Native to: South America, Mexico

Discovered by a French traveller around 1700 in the
mountain forests of Chile, the fuchsia has captivated
the horticultural world ever since. Over 2000 types of
fuchsia have been bred from the 100 or so wild
species; some are upright-growing, others pendulous,
and there is a huge variety of flower shapes and
colours. Those with small flowers are most suited for
training as bonsai – the majority already being well-
known as house plants. Fuchsias are evergreens with
soft, dark green leaves.

Site Inside throughout the year at a north-, east- or west-facing window or outside in a semi-shaded position from late spring. During winter the ideal temperature is around 8–12°C (46–54°F), although higher temperatures up to 18°C (64°F) are acceptable, in which case the plant must be stood somewhere very bright.

Watering If temperatures are high during summer, give plenty of water, otherwise keep evenly moist. During winter, if the site is a cool one, water sparingly; if warmer, use a little more water.

Feeding Every fortnight between spring and autumn using a liquid bonsai or houseplant food. In winter feed every four to six weeks, but only if the plant is in a warm position.

Repotting Every one or two years at the beginning of spring. At the same time trim the roots and prune the shoots back hard, right into the old wood.

Soil Loam, peat and sand mixture (1:1:1).

Pruning Branches at any time. New shoots must be continually cut back to leave two or three leaf pairs. If the plant is in bloom, only carry out an annual prune when repotting.

Wiring Usually not necessary, but if it is deemed so use extreme care. Small branches are very brittle.

Propagation Cuttings, taken in early summer.

Fuchsia fulgens hybrida
Fuchsia

Jacaranda mimosifolia, *approximately 9 years old and 36 cm (14 in) high. From the collection of Dr Gustavo Bataller, Spain.*

Family: Bignoniaceae
Native to: South America

An ornamental tree found in many a Mediterranean garden, the jacaranda has lovely fern-like leaves, which it sheds in autumn, and violet-blue flowers in spring. In its South American homeland it can grow up to 50 m (165 ft) tall. In bonsai form, jacarandas rarely bloom, but they make interesting little trees nevertheless.

Site Does not like blazing sunshine. It can be placed all year round in a bright window facing north, east or west; in winter it may be moved to a southerly window. Temperatures of 16–22°C (61–72°F) are required.

Watering Use softened water and keep evenly moist throughout the year – not too wet, and not too dry. Spray occasionally.

Feeding Every fortnight from spring to autumn using a liquid bonsai or houseplant food. Do not feed in winter.

Repotting Every one or two years in spring, along with root pruning.

Soil Loam, peat, sand mixture (1:2:2).

Pruning Branches possible at all times. Trim back new shoots to one or two leaf pairs once four pairs have developed. Alternatively, keep nipping out the shoot tips once new lateral shoots are showing.

Wiring Possible at any time, but new shoots may only be wired once they have become slightly woody.

Propagation Seeds.

**Jacaranda
mimosifolia**
Jacaranda

Lagerstroemia indica, *approximately 12 years old and 18 cm (7 in) high.*

Family: Lythraceae
Native to: Japan, Korea, China

Although an indigenous Asian plant, this subtropical shrub is grown in all Mediterranean countries. It is deciduous and has white, pink and lilac flowers. It is 3–7 m (10–23 ft) tall, has oval, light-green leaves and in late summer to early autumn produces flower panicles at the outer end of the first-year shoots. Older trees develop a vivid pinky-brown bark.

Site Indoors all year round at a sunny, airy, west- or south-facing window, but in strong sunlight provide some shade. Alternatively, place outside from late spring in a sunny location. During winter a cold-house climate of 6–10°C (43–50°F) is ideal, although somewhat higher temperatures will be tolerated.

Watering Give plenty in summer, but always allow the soil to dry out a certain amount before watering. Water less in winter. Also, be a bit more sparing with the water from the middle of summer, i.e. shortly before the flowering period, as this will encourage more flowers to form. If the plant does bloom, start giving ample water once more.

Feeding Every fortnight between spring and autumn using a liquid bonsai or houseplant food. Do not feed in winter.

Repotting Every two years in spring before new shoots appear. Trim the roots at same time.

Soil Loam, peat and sand mixture (1:2:1).

Pruning Branches at any time. Once the new shoots have formed six leaf pairs, prune back to leave only one or two. Such pruning is necessary in the shaping of young plants, and should also be carried out if it is not important that the plant flowers. Otherwise, wait until after the flowering period and prune back hard, right into the old wood.

Wiring May be carried out at any time except during the flowering period.

Propagation Seeds and cuttings.

Lagerstroemia indica
Indian Lilac, Chinese-crape Myrtle

Lantana camara, *approximately 8 years old and 40 cm (16 in) high.*

Family: Verbenaceae
Native to: Subtropical and tropical climatic regions

The lantana is an evergreen plant found in subtropical gardens where it forms very attractive, colourful hedging in its flowering period. Growing 1–2 m (3–6 ft) in height, *Lantana camara* is really a shrub with a smooth, light grey bark and dark green, oval leaves. In summer its flowers form round clusters and change colour from pink and yellow to orange and red. In many cases various colour combinations appear on the same plant, or flowers and blue-black berries may occur at the same time. In the Western world the lantana is familiar as a houseplant of many varieties which is easy to care for. It is highly suitable for bonsai training.

Site Either indoors all year round at a bright window facing east, west or south (in the latter case, shield from extremely bright sun), or outdoors from late spring until early autumn in an airy and sunny position. Winter temperature of 15–20°C (59–68°F) required. Lowering of temperature at night is important.

Watering Use water containing very little calcium. Water generously in summer, less so in winter, but keep evenly moist at all times.

Feeding Every fortnight from spring to autumn using a liquid bonsai or houseplant food. Feed every four to six weeks during winter.

Repotting Every two years in spring along with root pruning.

Soil Loam, peat, sand mixture (1:1:2).

Pruning Branches may be pruned at any time. New shoots should be left until after the flowering period then pruned back to one leaf pair. If you want fruits to develop, prune above the infructescences.

Wiring Possible at all times but unnecessary and unadvisable as *Lantana* branches are very brittle.

Propagation Cuttings and seeds.

Lantana camara
Lantana; Camara; Jamaica Mountain Sage; Surinam Tea Plant

Malpighia coccigera, *approximately 9 years old and 39 cm (15 in) high. From the collection of Jyoti and Nikunj Parekh, India.*

Family: Malpighiaceae
Native to: West Indies, subtropical climatic regions

A small, evergreen, thorny shrub with small, spiky, shiny-green leaves and small flowers in summer. Barbados Cherries grow at a striking rate but make highly decorative trees when trained as bonsai. Pale pink flowers appear at the leaf axils of lignified shoots.

Site All year round at a bright, sunny window facing east, west or south, but shield from sun that is too hot. Winter temperatures of 18–24°C (64–75°F) required.

Watering Keep evenly moist throughout the year.

Feeding Every fortnight from spring to autumn using a liquid bonsai or houseplant food; in winter every four to six weeks.

Repotting Every one or two years in spring, along with root pruning. A drainage layer of pebbles is important.

Soil Loam, peat and sand mixture (1:2:1).

Pruning Branches at any time. Prune back new shoots to one or two leaf pairs once five to six have formed.

Wiring Possible at all times with branches and slightly woody shoots. Do not bend older branches too much as they may split.

Propagation Seeds and cuttings, but leave to root in soil that is at a temperature of around 25°C (77°F).

Malpighia coccigera
Barbados Cherry

Murraya paniculata,
*approximately 48
years old and 55 cm
(22 in) high.*

Family: Rutaceae
Native to: Asia

Murraya paniculata
Jasmine Orange

An evergreen, tree-like shrub with a pale, smooth bark and unevenly pinnate leaves. Its white, bell-shaped flowers have a strong scent and its berries are red. Has a wide distribution in its tropical homeland of South China, India and Indonesia. Its bark is used in cosmetic preparations.

Site Indoors throughout the year. In summer it needs an airy, bright window facing east, west or south, but avoid leaving it standing in very bright sunshine and keep shaded if blazingly hot. Winter temperatures of 16–20°C (61–68°F), required.

Watering Keep evenly moist throughout the year.

Feeding Every fortnight in the main growing season between mid-spring and early autumn using a liquid indoor bonsai or houseplant food. Feed every four to six weeks during winter.

Repotting Every two years in spring along with root pruning.

Soil Loam, peat and sand mixture (2:2:1).

Pruning Branches at any time. Prune back new shoots to two leaves once four to six have formed.

Wiring Possible at any time in the year.

Propagation Seeds. Remove the red fruits from the pulp and sow immediately. Cuttings may also be used, but must be rooted in soil at a temperature of 28–30°C (82–86°F).

Myrciaria cauliflora,
*approximately 6
years old and 38 cm
(15 in) high.*

Family: Myrtaceae
Native to: Brazil, South America

In their tropical homeland, *Myrciaria* species grow
between 10 and 12 m (33–39 ft) high. They are fruit-
bearing shrubs that have the shape of a tree and a
great number of branches. The bark is quite vividly
speckled and the leaves quite long and pale green,
although leaves that grow subsequently are pink to
start with. During its flowering period *Myrciaria* is
covered in clusters of small white flowers all over its
trunk and along its branches. These eventually
develop into dark berries, which are sometimes sold
in delicatessens. The kernels of the fruits can be
grown as bonsai – they make pretty indoor trees but
rarely bloom in a temperate climate.

Site All year round at a bright window facing east,
west or north, but does not like brilliant sunshine.
Winter temperature of between 18 and 24°C
(64–75°F) required.

Watering Use water low in calcium content. Give
plenty of water during summer; winter amounts
required will vary, depending on location, but keep
evenly moist at all times.

Feeding Every fortnight from early spring to late
summer using a liquid bonsai or houseplant food.
During the winter feed every four to six weeks.

Repotting Every two years in spring, along with a
light pruning of the roots.

Soil Loam, peat and sand mixture (1:2:2).

Pruning Branches at any time. Cut back new growth
to leave two to four leaf pairs once four to five have
formed.

Wiring Usually not required, but can be carried out
at all times. Branches must be woody before wiring.

Propagation Seeds.

Myrtus communis,
*approximately 9
years old and 25 cm
(10 in) high.*

Family: Myrtaceae
Native to: Mediterranean area, Near East

An ornamental evergreen shrub of great charm, with dark green, leathery, lanceolate leaves. Between summer and autumn great numbers of small, white flowers grow in the leaf axils. A myrtle tree grows between 3 and 5 m (10–16 ft) high in its subtropical homeland, and since ancient times has been accorded great symbolic significance and legendary reputation. Europeans have known the myrtle since early in the Middle Ages, since when it has been used for medicinal purposes.

Myrtles are very good subjects for bonsai training because they grow vigorously and are easy to shape through pruning.

Myrtus communis
Myrtle

Site During summer they may be placed outside from late spring in a semi-shaded, airy spot or kept indoors by an easterly or westerly window. A south-facing window is too hot. From mid-autumn onwards the best location is somewhere cool but bright, with a temperature of 4–10°C (39–50°F). Myrtles can tolerate warmer temperatures, up to around 18°C (64°F), provided that the temperature is lowered at night.

Watering Abundantly in summer, sparingly in winter. Water containing little calcium is most suitable; and make sure the root area does not get waterlogged.

Feeding Every fortnight from early spring to late summer using a liquid indoor bonsai or houseplant food. In winter feed every four to six weeks if kept somewhere warm, otherwise cease feeding.

Repotting Every two to three years in spring along with root pruning. Do not press down too deeply into the new pot as the region where the trunk starts should be kept free of soil.

Soil Loam, peat and sand mixture (1:1:2).

Pruning Keep pruning the new branch growth back hard to leave two to three leaves. If you want the tree to flower, stop pruning from the middle of spring and only restart after the flowering period is over.

Wiring Branches may be wired at any time during the year, but can easily be shaped without any wiring.

Propagation Easy by means of cuttings (must be slightly woody) and seeds (which take a long time to germinate).

Olea europaea, approximately 80 years old and 50 cm (20 in) high. From the collection of Umberto Margiacchi, Italy.

Family: Oleaceae
Native to: Mediterranean region

Recognised as a characteristic Mediterranean tree since ancient times, its foliage gives the hills and valleys of the region a silvery-grey hue. Olives have narrow, elongated, grey-green, leathery leaves and develop unstriking flowers and black fruits. Some live to a great age; specimens known to be between 800 and 1000 years old are not uncommon. Gnarled branches and split trunks are characteristic of old olive trees.

Site Either indoors throughout the year at a bright, sunny window facing south or west, or outside from late spring in a sunny location. An airy, bright spot is best in winter, temperatures of 6–12°C (43–54°F) being ideal. Higher temperatures up to 18°C (64°F) can be endured, but do not forget to lower the temperature at night if this is the case.

Watering In summer and winter alike, allow the soil to get fairly dry, water thoroughly, then allow to dry again, and so on.

Feeding Every three to four weeks between mid-spring and early autumn using a liquid bonsai or houseplant food. Do not feed in winter.

Repotting Every two years in spring along with root pruning.

Soil Loam, peat and sand mixture (2:1:2).

Pruning Branches at all times, but do not prune too hard, as olive trees will start to grow too vigorously. Allow new shoots to develop six to eight leaf pairs then cut back to six pairs. Alternatively, let the new shoots grow really long and turn woody, then wire them and bend them into the desired shape.

Wiring Branches at all times; shoots only once they have become slightly woody.

Propagation Lignified cuttings or seeds (olive stones).

Olea europaea
Olive tree

Podocarpus
macrophyllus,
*approximately 120
years old and 68 cm
(27 in) high.*

Family: Podocarpaceae
Native to: Japan, China

Podocarpus
macrophyllus
Yew Podocarpus;
Kusamaki

In its native lands and in subtropical climatic regions, the yew podocarpus can reach a height of up to 12 m (39 ft). It is a conifer with horizontally growing branches. Slow-growing species.

Site Either indoors throughout the year at an east-, west- or north-facing window – not a south-facing one – or outside in a semi-shaded spot from late spring until early autumn. Keep indoors in winter at a temperature of 16–22°C (61–72°F).

Watering Moderately throughout the year, but keep evenly moist at all times.

Feeding Every fortnight between spring and autumn using a liquid bonsai or houseplant food. Feed every four to six weeks during winter.

Repotting Every two to three years in spring along with a very light pruning of the roots.

Soil Indoor bonsai earth or a loam, peat and sand mixture (1:1:1).

Pruning Branches may be pruned at any time. Trim back any new shoots to 2–4 cm ($\frac{3}{4}$–$1\frac{1}{2}$ in) after they have reached a length of 6–8 cm ($2\frac{1}{4}$–3 in), or allow new shoots to keep on growing and wire them once they have become slightly woody.

Wiring Branches at any time. New shoots between early autumn and early spring.

Propagation Seeds and cuttings.

Polyscias fruticosa,
*approximately 5
years old and 20 cm
(8 in) high.*

Family: Araliaceae   **Polyscias fruticosa**
Native to: Polynesia, tropical Asia

In their native lands, most aralia species grow as
shrubs which can reach considerable heights; some
have been familiar for a long time as pot plants. The
Ming aralia, an evergreen, is also suitable for bonsai
training. Its leaves are long-stalked, pinnate and
herbaceous – most effective when left to grow in its
natural habit, i.e. as a miniature shrub.

Site It can tolerate either a sunny or shaded position.
Keep indoors all year round at any window; it does
not matter which direction it faces. It need only be
shaded if the sun is blazingly hot. Winter
temperatures of 18–24°C (64–75°F) are required.
Never allow the temperature to drop below 16°C
(61°F).

Watering Keep moist at all times, but drain off any
excess water. Likes a high humidity level.

Feeding Every fortnight from spring to autumn using
a liquid bonsai or houseplant food. Apply every four
to six weeks during winter.

Repotting Every two years in spring along with root
pruning. Make sure drainage is adequate.

Soil Loam, peat and sand mixture (1:2:1).

Pruning Branches possible at any time. With new
shoots, either let them continue to grow then prune
back hard the following spring, or keep trimming
them back to leave one or two leaf pairs as soon as
four to five pairs have formed.

Wiring May be carried out at any time, but never
very effective.

Propagation Cuttings, allowed to root in soil heated
to a temperature of 22–24°C (72–75°F).

Punica granatum
'Nana',
approximately 12
years old and 35 cm
(14 in) high.

Family: Punicaceae
Native to: Mediterranean region, Iran, India

Pomegranate trees have been cultivated since
prehistoric times. In ancient Egypt and ancient Israel
it was considered a sacred plant to be worshipped. It
was said to have 613 pips – just as the Old
Testament contains 613 laws. Pomegranates are
shrubs that grow like trees; they are deciduous and
have small, pointed, shiny green leaves, orange-red
flowers that appear in late summer, and small, red,
apple-like fruits. In temperate latitudes the fruit buds
rarely ripen and usually fall off along with the leaves.

Site Either all year round indoors at a well-ventilated southerly or westerly window, or outside from late spring until early autumn in a sunny position; once the leaves have fallen, bring back indoors again. The plant may be overwintered at either a coolish or relatively warm temperature, i.e. 6–10°C, or up to 18°C (43–50°F, or up to 64°F). With the warmer temperatures, however, the plant will grow less compact, and more spindly.

Watering Give plenty of water in summer, very little in winter if the plant undergoes a dormant period. Keep evenly moist if you have chosen a somewhat warmer site.

Feeding Between spring and autumn. During the main growing period feed every fortnight with a liquid bonsai or houseplant food. If kept in a warm location over winter, feed every four to six weeks, otherwise do not feed.

Repotting Every two years in spring before new shoots start to appear. Prune roots at same time.

Soil Loam, peat and sand mixture (1:1:1).

Pruning Branches at any time. Allow new shoots to develop six leaf pairs then trim back to leave one or two. If flowers are wanted, do not prune new growth after the beginning of spring, but prune hard once the flowering period is over in order to retain the tree shape.

Wiring Not during the flowering period, otherwise at any time.

Propagation Cuttings and seeds.

Punica granatum
'Nana'
Pomegranate tree

Rhododendron
simsii, *syn.* Azalea
indica, *approximately
65 years old and
68 cm (27 in) high.*

Family: Ericaceae
Native to: Far East

Evergreen, beautifully-coloured, flowering shrubs,
rhododendrons are found in the cool, damp, shaded
valleys of their subtropical homelands. The small-
flowered dwarf types are most suitable as
houseplants and bonsai. They have small, shiny
leaves that range from light to dark green in colour,
and the flowers that bloom between mid-autumn
and mid-spring come in a huge variety of colours,
every conceivable shade of white, pink, red, orange
and violet.

Site Prefers a fairly cool position throughout the year. During the summer it should be placed in a cool, bright window facing north, east or west (shade if necessary), or outside from late spring to early autumn in a semi-shaded spot. Requires a bright window site during winter with a temperature of 6–12°C (43–54°F).

Watering Use water that contains little calcium. Give plenty in summer, particularly during the flowering period. Otherwise, water moderately, but keep evenly moist. Do not allow to become over-dry and also avoid waterlogging.

Feeding Every fortnight from mid-summer to late summer using a bonsai or organic houseplant food. Do not feed in winter.

Repotting About every two to three years after flowering, along with a light root pruning.

Soil Loam, peat and sand mixture (1:4:2).

Pruning Branches may be pruned at any time. Any shoots that start to form around the flower buds should be nipped out completely. After flowering, the flower remains should be removed to stop the plant forming seeds, instead of which it will start to produce new shoots more vigorously. Keep pruning new shoots back to leave one or two leaf pairs once about six pairs have formed. New shoots growing directly on the trunk and at the root area should be removed immediately.

Wiring Azalea twigs are very brittle, so any wiring must be carried out very carefully.

Propagation Cuttings, but difficult.

Rhododendron simsii
Azalea

Sageretia theezans,
*approximately 35
years old and 42 cm
(17 in) high. From
the collection of Yee-
sun Wu, Hong Kong.*

Family: Rhamnaceae
Native to: Southern China

A tropical, evergreen shrub with small, shiny, pale-green leaves and an interesting, strikingly flecked bark, similar to the bark of a plane tree. It is a prodigious grower, highly suited to bonsai training and to being kept indoors. During winter it survives very well indoors at temperatures of between 18 and 22°C (64–72°F), provided that the humidity is sufficiently high.

Site Either indoors all year round at a bright window facing east, west or south or outside from late spring. Nevertheless, both inside and out, it should be kept slightly shaded if the sun is very hot. In winter a bright position is also required, ideally with a temperature of 12–18°C (54–64°F) although a higher range of 18–24°C (64–75°F) is equally acceptable. In the latter case spray your plant every other day.

Watering In summer give plenty. In winter the amount given will depend on location, but keep evenly moist in any case.

Feeding After new shoots have formed, feed every fortnight from spring to autumn with a liquid bonsai or houseplant food. If placed somewhere warm during winter feed once a month.

Repotting Every one or two years before new growth starts to appear in the spring. Prune roots at the same time.

Soil Loam, peat and sand mixture (2:2:1).

Pruning Branches may be pruned throughout the year. Cut back any new shoots to two or three leaf pairs. If the *Sagaretia* is not pruned, delicate, yellowy-white flower panicles will develop in the leaf axils of the new shoots.

Wiring Branches at any time. New shoots only once they have become woody.

Propagation Easy, using cuttings.

Sagaretia theezans
Sagaretia

81

Schefflera
actinophylla,
*approximately 10
years old and 45 cm
(18 in) high
(including rock).*

Family: Araliaceae
Native to: Australia

In tropical countries the Umbrella tree grows up to
15 m (50 ft) tall. It is a shady, evergreen with almost
umbrella-sized leaves at the end of long stalks. It has
long been a favourite pot plant among Europeans.
The trunk of a *Schefflera* stays relatively thin and
unlike other tropical shrubs it does not branch out
to form a crown. As a bonsai, the *Schefflera* is often
used for rock planting as it forms mangrove-like
roots. Once the trunk has reached the height that
complements the rock, the tops of the shoots should
be chopped off. The plant will subsequently form

new shoots. Repeated pruning of this sort will encourage the plant to branch out, as well as keeping it compact and allowing thicker roots to develop.

Schefflera actinophylla
Australian Umbrella Tree

Site Indoors all year round at as bright a window as possible – the brighter it is, the shorter the leaf stalks and the smaller the leaves. The ideal temperature range is 18–22°C (64–72°F), and it should never be allowed to fall below 15°C (59°F). *Schefflera* may be kept directly above a radiator. If left somewhere too dark the leaf stalks will grow too long, and if the plant is kept too moist the leaves will grow too big.

Watering If the plant is sited on a rock stood on a layer of pebbles, this layer must be kept moist at all times. Never stand the rock in water. If the tree is growing in soil, water sparingly.

Feeding Once a month using a liquid bonsai or houseplant food. Use the strength given for pot plants. With a rock planting spread some hydroponic fertiliser under the layer of pebbles: one tablespoon is enough for six months.

Repotting Every two years in late winter or early spring for *Scheffleras* growing in soil; roots should be pruned at the same time. With rock bonsai positioned on top of a layer of pebbles, the roots can also be trimmed if the tree has grown a great deal. If the rock has become too small for the plant, transfer it to a bonsai dish filled with earth.

Soil Loam, peat and sand mixture (1:2:2).

Pruning Possible at any time in the year.

Wiring Not possible.

Propagation Seeds may be sown in spring, or cuttings may be taken throughout the year.

Serissa foetida,
*approximately 6
years old and 25 cm
(10 in) high.*

Family: Rubiaceae
Native to: Southern China, South-east Asia

'Tree of a Thousand Stars' is the common Chinese
name for *Serissa*. An evergreen, *Serissa* is a prolific
grower with small leaves and white flowers that
appear in mid-summer; the occasional flower crops
up at any time during the year. To encourage more
blooms to appear, flowers that have withered should
be nipped out the moment they are spotted. *Serissa*
often reacts badly to a change of site by shedding
much of its foliage, but it will quickly recover.

Site In summer either keep indoors at a very bright window facing east or west, even south (but must then be shaded from very strong sunlight), or place outside from late spring, but away from the full glare of the sun. During winter place by a bright window and keep at a temperature of between 12 and 18°C (54–64°F). If the temperature is lowered at night, somewhat higher temperatures may also be endured.

Watering In summer this plant requires a lot of water. In winter keep it evenly moist. Should branches begin to die, the cause can often be traced to damage in the root area as a result of the soil drying out into clumps. Sometimes too much fertiliser may be the cause.

Feeding Every fortnight from spring to autumn, preferably using purely organic fertilisers (liquid bonsai or houseplant foods). In winter only feed if the plant has been placed somewhere warm, approximately every four to six weeks.

Repotting Every two years in spring along with a light root pruning. When the roots are cut you will notice a penetrating smell, which explains its specific name *foetida*, Latin for 'stinking'.

Soil Loam, sand and peat mixture (1:1:1).

Pruning Branches may be pruned throughout the year. Trim back young shoots to one or two leaf pairs once three or four pairs have formed. To maintain the compact appearance of the tree, it should in addition be pruned back hard every one or two years right into the old wood. After pruning, the new growth that forms will usually develop flowers, once two or three pairs of leaves have been produced.

Wiring May be carried out at any time.

Propagation Very easy, using cuttings.

Serissa foetida
Serissa: Tree of a Thousand Stars

Ulmus parvifolia,
*approximately 30
years old and 46 cm
(18 in) high.*

Family: Ulmaceae
Native to: China

In their Asiatic homeland, these lovely, semi-
evergreen trees can grow up to 20 m (65 ft) tall,
although the Chinese have long cultivated them in
miniature form. Elm bonsai have a very attractive
branching shape and oval-shaped, crenated leaves
that have a fresh green colour. They are very easy
trees to take care of and can withstand temperature
variations, even if they are being kept too wet or too
dry.

Site Indoors throughout the year at a bright, even sunny location (any window will do, east-, west-, north- or south-facing). Alternatively place outdoors from late spring; the actual site may be anything from semi-shaded to sunny. During winter may be kept in a cool spot at 6–10°C (43–50°F) or in a fairly warm one, 18–22°C (64–72°F).

Watering Water thoroughly in summer, leave to dry out slightly, then water thoroughly once more, and so on. In winter, the amount given will depend on location; if in a warm spot, continue as for summer; if somewhwere cooler, use less water but give some regularly.

Feeding Every fortnight between spring and autumn using a liquid bonsai or houseplant food. Feed every four to six weeks during winter.

Repotting Every two years at the beginning of spring along with root pruning.

Soil Loam, peat and sand mixture (2:1:1).

Pruning Branches may be pruned at any time. Allow new shoots to develop eight leaf pairs, then trim back to leave two or three.

Wiring Branches at all times; shoots only once they have become slightly woody.

Propagation Easy, using lignified cuttings.

Ulmus parvifolia
Chinese Elm

Pests and Diseases

A healthy plant is able to resist attack by the majority of pests and diseases, so the best way of protecting your specimens is to make sure to take meticulous care of them. This will include choosing the right site, getting the composition of the soil rights, as well as watering and feeding correctly. If then any plant falls ill or is attacked by pests, the first thing to do is to consider whether you are caring for it correctly. Do not just fight the disease, but also look for its cause.

Every amateur gardener knows that too much light, heat or humidity can be just as harmful as too little. A lack of water in the soil, for example, may cause the plant to wither or the edges of its leaves to dry up, deformities may appear in the stem, leaves or flowers, the flowers may be shed altogether, the plant may stop growing prematurely, or a host of other problems may ensue. Too much water and waterlogging may impede soil ventilation and consequently upset the balance of the soil, in which case the plant's roots may be unable to function properly and may even start to rot, leaves may turn yellow or the whole plant might actually die.

This chapter should help you in the correct diagnosis of disease symptoms and in the recognition of pests, which will in turn mean that you can treat them effectively, a task made more and more easy with today's modern treatments.

Recently, it is the easy-to-use granule preparations that have been gaining in popularity. The granules are sprinkled over the surface of the soil, when the plant is watered the granules dissolve and are absorbed by the roots. The active ingredients disperse throughout the plant to be sucked up by the pests. Provided that the humidity level is high enough, you should start to see results within three to seven days.

Sprays can also help in the fight against pests. They are effective against fungal and animal pests, in particular mildew, aphids, spider mites and white fly.

Aphids

Atrophied leaves and shoots are often one sign of aphids. They can usually be found on the undersides of leaves and on buds, and they literally suck the plant dry. Aphids can nearly always be removed simply by spraying them away with a jet of water, but if this does not do the trick use a garden spray such as pirimicarb, or use malathion or fenitrothion. Alternatively, a systemic such as dimethoate will prove effective.

Scale insects

Brown, pock-like swellings on the undersides of leaves are almost certainly signs of an attack by scale insects. They can be scraped off with a stick, or simply rubbed off with the hand. If this does not work, use a systemic such as dimethoate, or you can spray your tree several times with a 0.15 per cent malathion emulsion.

Woolly aphids

A kind of small cotton wool ball growing on the trunk, in the fork of a branch or at the junction between leaf and branch is the unmistakable sign of woolly aphids. These tiny creatures sit cocooned inside a waxy deposit right at the heart of the woolly balls, well protected against any methods of treatment. Prise the woolly balls apart, and then treat the same way as for aphids.

Root aphids

Yellowing leaves and a general wasting of the tree can sometimes be caused by aphids attacking the root system. To check, lift the tree out of its dish and look for tiny, greyish-white growths, a little like cotton wool balls, along the roots. The recommended treatment is a solution of metasystox poured directly onto the soil.

Red spider mite	A filmy spider's web that makes the leaves look paler is often the sign of the red spider mite. You can see the mites by holding a sheet of white paper under an infected branch and shaking it. They look like red paprika powder usually, although sometimes they can be yellow or brown in colour, but under a microscope they are recognisable as insects. Spray with malathion or pirimiphos-methyl two or three times, with a fortnight between each spray. Alternatively, try a systemic such as dimethoate.

White fly	Lantanas, hibiscus and sageretias are particularly prone to attack by the white, scaly moth insect known as white fly. Its eggs and larvae lie hidden on the undersides of the leaves on the stricken plant. The damage they cause by sucking on the leaves becomes evident when the upper side of the leaves start to look dotted with yellow. White fly is best treated with malathion, bioresmethrin or dimethoate (systemic).

Diseases

Root rot	If the leaves start to turn brown and whole branches die, it is often a case of root rot. It can be caused by overfeeding, but more commonly it occurs when the tree has been allowed to stand in water. The delicate fibrous roots die, start to rot and become slimy. First remove all rotted pieces of root, then dip the remaining healthy roots in a benomyl solution to prevent more rotting.

Next, repot the plant in some new soil and water thoroughly, but from then on water more sparingly than before. This is to allow new roots to form – a plant with damaged roots cannot absorb as much water as a healthy one. Do not feed your plant for at least eight weeks. While the tree is recovering, keep it out of direct sunlight – it needs tender treatment!

| | **Black spot** |

f you find sooty, black deposits, usually on older eaves and on one side only, your bonsai will amost ertainly be suffering from black spot. It is a disease hat is often associated with an aphid attack. The condition can be treated with an insecticide.

| | **Powdery mildew** |

This is identifiable as a white, floury coating on the upper sides of leaves. A fungal disease, it occurs when there is insufficient air circulation around your plant or when the plant has been sprayed too late in the evening for the leaves to be able to dry out before the onset of night. Occasionally, a fertiliser too rich in nitrogen can be the cause. Mildew needs to be treated with a fungicide such as benomyl or any sulphur-based fungicide.

| | **Downy mildew** |

A grey mouldy coating on the underside of a leaf and yellow flecks on the upper side are usually the signs of downy mildew. Either the air circulation around the plant is not good enough or the humidity in both air and soil is too high. More air should be allowed to get at the plant and it should be sprayed with a fungicide.

| | **Chlorosis** |

The sign of this disease is yellowing of the leaves although the leaf veins stay green, the cause being a lack of iron. It can be rectified by adding chelated iron when watering.

Household remedies

1) Stinging nettles. For cold extracts place 100 g (3½ oz) of fresh stinging nettle in 1 litre (1¾ pints) of water. Use undiluted to treat aphids and white fly.

2) Herbal teas, e.g. wormwood. Pour 1 litre of boiling water over 3 g of dried wormwood. Leave to draw for 15 minutes, strain, allow to cool then use undiluted in the treatment of aphids, mites and mildew.

3) A soft soap solution (5 g of soap to 1 litre of water) may be used to cleanse stricken plants, but make sure the solution does not come into contact with the root ball.

Important points regarding the treatment of pests and diseases

Taking meticulous care of the specimens is the best form of protection. Special treatments to combat nearly all types of pest and disease are readily available.

Follow the instructions exactly as given on the packing. Do not spray your plants indoors. With aerosol cans spray from the height recommended in the instructions to avoid frost damage from the propulsive gas.

Do not just treat pests and diseases; look for their causes too!

If you are not sure what is ailing your plant, ask an expert before trying any form of treatment.

Repotting and Root Pruning

No indoor bonsai will stay at its best if kept in the same soil over a number of years. This is because the soil becomes poor, meaning that it contains fewer of the substances needed by the tree. The pH value of the soil alters and it becomes less permeable to air and water; and gradually the soil is used up, leaving in its place a matted network of roots with hardly any earth surrounding it.

So the main thing to remember with repotting is that you are providing good, new earth along with root pruning – transferring the plant into a new pot or dish is of secondary importance. To keep a good balance between the roots and the crown of the tree, the roots will have to be cut back by at least a third. At the same time take the opportunity to remove any dead bits of root. Having done this, the root system will be able to develop evenly again, the formation of new fibrous roots being particularly marked.

Root pruning.

The same dish can be used for repotting elderly indoor bonsai, unless you want to change it for aesthetic reasons. Young and fast-growing plants, however, will need a new dish roughly 2 cm ($\frac{3}{4}$ in) bigger than the old every one or two years.

Frequency of repotting

How often you will have to repot indoor bonsai will depend on the age and species of the plant. Fast-growing and fairly young trees should be repotted once a year. Older specimens and very slow-growing ones will last two or three years in the same soil.

It is high time to repot your plant and prune its roots once the soil is riddled with roots and the root ball itself has been pushed up rather high.

Earth ball packed with roots – high time to repot.

The right time to repot is at the beginning of spring before the main growing season has begun. However, most tropical species of bonsai may be repotted at any time of the year.

Apart from the function of providing the plant with a means of support, the soil also performs the important task of providing food for it.

Soil is a mixture of organic and inorganic particles, its most important components being loam, sand and humus. Loam (a naturally-occurring mixture of sand and clay) has a buffer action. Sand breaks the soil up and makes it more permeable for air and water (a drainage effect). The humus content provides among other things a fertile base for vital bacteria to grow. Humus is contained in peat, for example, and in forest soil.

Soil is suitable for indoor bonsai can be bought from shops ready-mixed and packed. One that can be recommended is made up of 30 per cent clay, 40 per cent peat, 145 per cent bark humus and 15 per cent bits of pumice. It is also enriched with nutrients and trace elements. As the pH value of this particular soil mixture is between 5.5 and 6.5, it is acceptable to almost every species of indoor bonsai. Azaleas are perhaps an obvious exception – this soil would not be acidic enough for them, and you would have to add some acidic peat. If you prefer to make up your own soil mixture, use fresh peat, compost and sand in the ratio 2:1:2. The peat and sand can be bought, and for the compost use John Innes No. 2 (this must be sieved to remove all fine particles). For azaleas and other species that require acidic soil change the mixture to one part loam, two parts sand and five parts peat.

Repotting technique   Once you have decided to repot, allow the soil to dry
out a bit more than usual as this will make it easier
to loosen the earth from the roots.

1) Remove the tree from
its pot.

2) If you are transferring to a new pot, cover the
drainage holes with a piece of plastic mesh secured
with a loop of wire to
prevent it slipping. This
stops any soil trickling out.

3) If you have chosen a very shallow pot that might
not provide enough support for the tree, push some
wire through the drainage holes so that you can use it
later to secure the tree in place. Usually this is not
necessary with indoor bonsai as the tree will not be
put outside after repotting and so is not exposed to
wind or other adverse
conditions.

4) If you are planting your tree in a very deep pot,
include a drainage layer to avoid water build-up.
Cover the bottom of the pot with coarse gravel or
pebbles up to a depth of
about 2 cm (¾ in) before
adding any earth.

2cm

) Take a handful of soil from the
mixture you have already
prepared and place it on the
bottom of the dish or on
the layer of gravel.

) Carefully loosen the old
soil from the roots
using a piece of stick.

) Next prune the roots back by
about a third to a half.

) Now place your bonsai in the pot, but not right
in the middle. Make sure the root area does not show
over the edge of the pot. To improve its appearance
gently spread the roots out evenly in all directions.

Any particularly wayward
roots can be held firmly in
place with a wire clip.

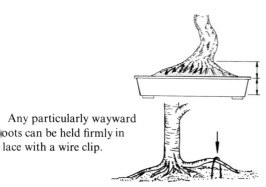

9) If you have threaded some wire through the drainage holes, now secure your tree with it.

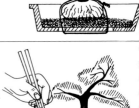

10) Add the soil to the pot, using a stick to work it into the spaces between the roots. Firm gently along the edge of the pot so as not to compact the compost.

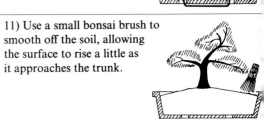

11) Use a small bonsai brush to smooth off the soil, allowing the surface to rise a little as it approaches the trunk.

After repotting, water your tree very carefully, making sure none of the soil is washed away, or stand the pot up to half its depth in water. Do not feed the plant for at least four weeks and water more sparingly than usual. This is because pruned roots ca absorb less water and food for a while after repottin

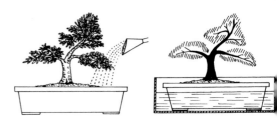

You will need the following.
The correct soil mixture – either bought ready-
prepared or prepared by yourself.
Coarse gravel, if required.
Plastic mesh.
Bonsai wire, if required.
A large pair of bonsai scissors.
A piece of stick.
A larger pot, if required.
A bonsai brush (not vital).

You must repot if the roots of the tree have virtually
swallowed up the soil. Before placing the tree in new
soil, prune the roots back by about a third. Older
specimens can usually be repotted in the same pot.
Young and tropical species need to be repotted
about every one or two years, older ones every three
or four. The best time to repot is the beginning of
spring. After repotting do not feed the plant for four
weeks and water more sparingly.

Shaping Indoor Bonsai

Bonsai trees acquire their shape by control of their growth. They are not intended to grow tall, but they should look strong and sturdy. The crown should look compact, with lots of small shoots rather than a few long ones. In essence, an indoor bonsai should look like a healthy, natural tree that has remained small because of certain prevailing conditions, because that is exactly what it is.

To keep the right proportions between branch and leaf, flower and fruit, keep pruning your tree, nipping out unwanted flowers and sometimes wiring it. If you do not step in to control the shape in which the tree will grow, your specimen will not achieve that special beauty so characteristic of bonsai.

As many indoor bonsai continue to grow throughout the year, you will usually have to shape your tree more often than outdoor varieties.

First of all decide in what style you want to train your tree. There are many different basic styles, all of which are found in nature. Choose as a model the shape that best suits your specimen. Place the tree somewhere level with your eyes so that you are not looking down at it, but directly into it. In this way you can see the shape that already exists within the tree, recognise any particular features it may have, and decide which part you want to be the front and which the back.

If you are still unsure what your tree has to offer, look for ideas in the way the tree grows in nature.

Formal upright
Branches grow evenly in all
directions, although the front of the
tree is kept free of branches up to
the top third.

Informal upright
Trunk winds round in curves that
become smaller towards the top.
Branches grow only on the outer
curves.

Twisted trunk
Trunk tapers towards the top and
twists round and round on itself.
Various directions of growth are
possible.

Exposed root
Roots form the lower part of the
trunk. Mangrove trees with their
adventitious roots are the
inspiration for this style.

101

Weeping willow
A more or less upright tree with hanging branches.

Broom
Upright trunk with branches spreading out on all sides from a particular height. Reminiscent of a giant up-ended broom.

Umbrella
Many tropical trees have enormous, umbrella-like crowns that cast shade over a wide area.

Conical
Slender, strictly upright trees such as cypresses.

Spherical
Dense network of branches growing on an upright trunk making a spherical crown.

Literati
Trunk grows in an informal upright style or slightly inclined, with branches only in the top third.

Windswept
Trunk at an angle with branches and twigs growing in one direction only – as if lashed by the wind.

Slanting
Similar to the windswept style except that the branches grow in all directions. Strong roots are exposed in the direction of incline.

Semi-cascade

Models in nature: trees that jut out horizontally above a cliff. The top of the tree lies level with the edge of the pot or a bit lower.

Cascade

Models in nature: trees that hang down low over a rock. Trunk and branches of the bonsai hang down well beyond the edge of a usually tall pot.

Twin trunk

Two trunks of different widths growing from one root, the styling of their branches blending perfectly with each other.

Clump

Several trunks growing from one root to form a small group of trees.

Raft
Trunk buried horizontally in a pot which then grows roots. Branches then trained to grow upwards producing the effect of individual trees.

Multi-tree
Several miniature trees of the same species but of differing ages, heights and trunk widths planted in a very shallow pot.

Rock-grown
Trees take root on a rock in small hollows or crevices.

Root-over-rock
Tree's roots climb over the rock and down into the soil in the pot.

Pruning of branches and twigs

By pruning the branches of your tree you are in fact determining the basic shape of your bonsai. No matter which style you have chosen, the branches shown in the diagram below should be removed in every case.

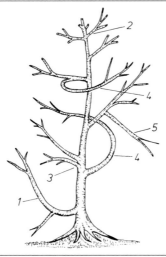

1) Branches in the lower third of the front of the tree, the front meaning that side of the tree from which it is easiest to look into the heart of the plant and from where you can see as much of the structure of the trunk and branches as possible. On a bonsai the branches should never grow forwards but always to the sides or to the rear. It is only in the upper part of the crown that small branches and twigs are allowed to grow forwards, largely for artistic reasons.

2) One of two branches growing opposite each other at the same height on the trunk.

3) One of two branches growing directly one on top of the other.

4) Branches that grow from one side of the tree, across the trunk to the other side.

5) Branches growing downwards.

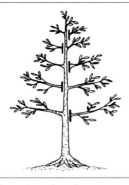

One of two branches growing opposite each other is removed.

These are not intended to be strict rules; they are merely guidelines. They hold good for most styles of bonsai, but not all.

Branch and twig pruning is the most important aspect of giving shape to your tree, so take enough time over it. Cover with your hand the branch you intend to remove and see if you can imagine how its removal will alter the proportions and overall appearance of the tree.

Do not be over-cautious! Pruning your tree to leave only the most significant branches enhances its character.

How to prune branches and twigs

The right tool will make the job easier.

1) Thin branches should be snipped off directly at the trunk using a pair of bonsai scissors.

2) Concave-cutting pliers are best for the removal of thicker branches. They leave behind a concave incision that heals quickly with little scarring.

Ulmus parvifolia, *approximately 20 years old and 40 cm (16 in) high.*

3) Very thick branches need in the first instance to be sawn off roughly. Concave-cutting pliers are best for getting rid of the end bit. Large wounds should be sealed with grafting wax.

Pruning shoots and leaves

Shoots should only develop where a new branch is intended to grow. If one forms where you do not want it, cut it off. To give your bonsai shape and to keep it in the style you want, any new shoots will have to be trimmed continually. Pruning of new growth also helps keep your tree strong and healthy. You will be allowing more light and air to reach it, helping to create a more delicate network of branches, limiting the length to which the branches will grow and strengthening those branches growing in the lower part of the tree. In addition, by pruning the shoots you will also determine the direction in which subsequent branches will grow, simply

because the direction of growth of the previous leaf axil – i.e. the axil left behind after pruning – is also the direction in which the subsequent shoot will grow. This method of shaping bonsai by pruning alone is known as 'cut and grow'.

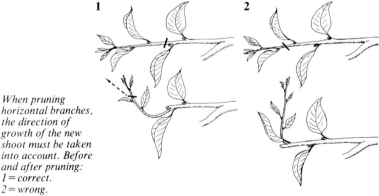

When pruning horizontal branches, the direction of growth of the new shoot must be taken into account. Before and after pruning:
1 = correct.
2 = wrong.

As many indoor bonsai are native to tropical countries, they grow throughout the year, and so their shoots may be pruned or removed at any time. For others, particularly subtropical species, the main growing season is from spring to autumn and so they should only be pruned during that period. The only exceptions are those subtropical indoor species that are kept at a higher temperature over winter, as they will of course continue to grow even at that time of year. *Flowering bonsai* should only be pruned after the flowering period is over.

Leaves are pruned less often than shoots. Any individual leaves that get too big should be removed during the growing season. All other leaves should only be pruned, if necessary, once a year sometime between early spring and late summer. Leaf pruning has three aims.

1) A fine branching of the tree. This is brought about because after pruning a new shoot will grow from the bud on the leaf stipule.

2) Reduction in size of the leaves, which have usually grown too big in relation to the rest of the tree. This helps enhance the tree's natural beauty and creates a more harmonious effect.

3) Thinning out of the crown. This is also important for allowing light and air to reach the inner branches, without which they would slowly die.

In order not to shock the tree too much, do not cut all its leaves at once; remove the biggest ones first, and the others a week or two later. If possible, leave the stalks, as this will prevent damage to the bud lying at the junction of the branch and leaf axil. Remember also that after having its leaves pruned the tree will require less water as it will be losing less through evaporation.

How to prune shoots and leaves

As a rule, allow new shoots to develop four to six leaves or leaf pairs, then prune them back to one to three leaves or pairs. Alternatively, keep nipping out the leaf buds.

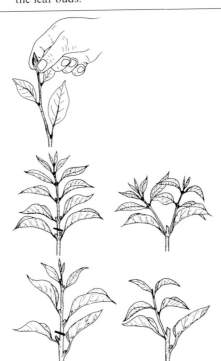

Nipping out of buds.

Before and after pruning of shoots: in leaves growing opposite one another.

In leaves following an alternating pattern.

Try to prune leaves so that at least a small part of the stalk remains.

More precise instructions are given in the descriptions of the individual plants on pages 32–87.

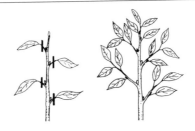

Before and after leaf pruning.

f the lower part of the trunk is too thin in relation o the crown, leave the lower branches attached, ven though they would normally be removed. The etention of the branches accelerates nutrient xchange and with it the growth of the trunk. After bout a year the trunk should be as thick as you vant it. In a similar way you can thicken branches nd twigs that are too thin by not removing any hoots or leaves over a temporary period, for the nore leaves there are on a branch the more food it vill take up, and the quicker its circumference will ncrease. If a branch gets too thick, remove all its eaves once or twice a year, and do not carry out any eaf pruning on the remaining branches.

To make the branch grow thicker twigs are not cut off.

Pruning aerial roots Aerial roots are a typical characteristic of many tropical plants, such as *Ficus* and *Schefflera*. They give an exotic appearance to indoor bonsai, and for many keepers of bonsai they form an essential part of the overall shape of their specimens, being trained to grow along the trunk and branches and down into the soil.

Schefflera arboricola, from the collection of David Fukumoto, Hawaii. The aerial roots enhance the exotic effect of this specimen.

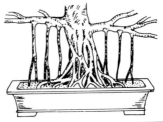

Aerial roots trained to grow parallel to the trunk and down into the soil.

You can happily let the roots grow down into the soil as they will help provide additional food for your tree.

You will not damage your bonsai by cutting off its aerial roots, although it is advisable only to remove those ones that spoil the overall appearance.

You will need the following.

A strong pair of bonsai scissors for cutting branches
and aerial roots. It is all right to use the same pair of
scissors used for root pruning.

A slender pair of bonsai scissors for trimming
shoots.

Leaf cutters.

Concave-cutting pliers.

A bonsai saw for sawing off very thick branches.

Grafting wax.

New shoots should be continually pruned in order
to style the tree as desired. Branches and shoots may
be pruned throughout the year, but flowering trees
should only be pruned after the flowering period is
over. Leaves should be nipped out or cut off once a
year, but only if this is considered necessary. If at all
possible, do not prune all the leaves at once. Only
prune aerial roots if they spoil the exotic appearance
of your tropical specimens.

Wiring

With many species of indoor bonsai the old Chinese maxim 'Let it grow then prune' is good enough advice for achieving the desired style. Nevertheless there are some that will have to be wired as well.

Next to pruning, wiring is the most important technique in the training of bonsai. The use of wires is the quickest way of styling your tree, as wire makes branches and twigs pliable and holds them firmly in the desired position for as long as is required for the trunk and branches to set.

New shoots always grow towards light, usually upwards. By wiring you can very carefully correct this natural direction of growth.

To master the technique of wiring you need not only patience but also a bit of skill and a certain amount of practice. If you are a beginner in terms of bonsai growing, choose plants that do not need any fundamental change to their basic shape. Practise wiring by trying to make small changes in direction on branches or twigs before daring to tackle bigger things. With experience you will be able to make the whole tree bend in a different way or make it appear older by bending its branches down.

Small corrective measures can be undertaken at any time during the growing season – with most indoor species this means at any time during the year. As a basic rule new shoots should only be wired once they are matured, meaning that they have hardened slightly – a horticulturist would say they have turned 'woody'. More major alterations to shape should not really be attempted during the main growing period.

The wire should not grow into the trunk or branches. With fast-growing species, *Ficus* spp. for example, this can easily happen within three to four weeks. That is why it is better to keep the wire loose rather than tight, as the bark on many indoor bonsai is sensitive and easily damaged. Inspect the areas that have been wired regularly and, if necessary, loosen the wire a little early even if the desired new shape has not quite been achieved. No harm is done to the tree by wiring it two or three times one after the other, but a great deal of damage might be done f wire that had become embedded was torn out. If, despite all the care, a piece of wire did become embedded in the bark, only remove those bits of wire that are free – using a pair of wire cutters – and leave the ingrown wire in the tree. There are lots of examples of lovely, old trees that are healthy despite having wire embedded in them.

Should a small tear or split appear in a branch that is being bent with wires, it should be sealed immediately with grafting wax; larger tears need to be bound with raffia.

You need only wire a few branches to make all the branches on a tree grow more evenly. This is because the gap between the branches becomes greater, enabling more air and light to reach the inner branches as well. Wiring does not inhibit the growth of your tree, with one exception: if you train a branch to grow downwards it will develop a bit more slowly.

How to wire your tree

1) For the trunk you will need a fairly thick piece of wire; for branches and twigs a somewhat thinner one. Use anodised aluminium or copper wire that has been prepared by annealing.

2) Take one end of the wire and push it at an angle down to the bottom of the pot starting from the back of the tree at the beginning of the trunk.

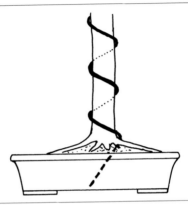

3) Even if you only intend wiring a single branch, the branch opposite should also be wired to give the wire added support. Start in the middle, i.e. at the branch or trunk that joins onto the one to be wired.

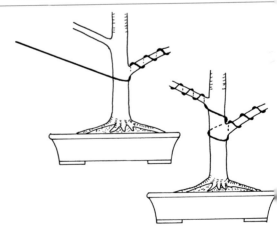

4) Whether it is the trunk, branch or twig to be wired, the wire should be wound in the direction of growth, i.e. spirally going from bottom to top. The distance between each coil of wire should remain constant. It is better to wind the wire round fairly loosely, as that is usually enough to shape the branch.

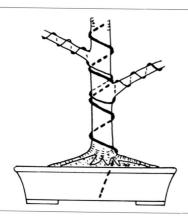

5) Make sure not to trap any leaves under the wire.

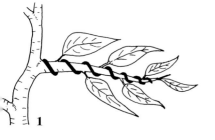

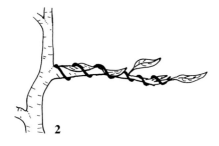

Be careful not to trap leaves under your wire!

1 = correct.
2 = wrong.

6) Before wiring remove any branches that grow downwards.

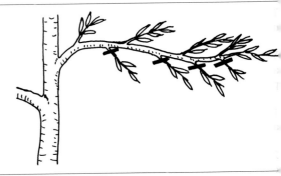

7) Lastly, once you have wired the branches carefully bend them into shape.

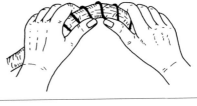

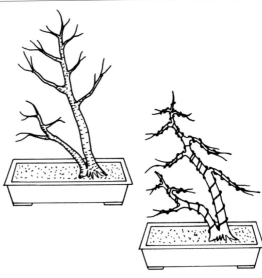

A bonsai before and after wiring.

The wiring technique needs to be learned. Start by making small corrections to the direction of growth.

You will need the following: bonsai wire (anodised aluminium or copper) in various thicknesses and a pair of wire cutters.

1) Wind the wire round the selected branch evenly in a spiral, following the natural direction of growth.

2) Do not bind the wire too tightly. Indoor bonsai often have a very sensitive bark.

3) The wire should not cut into the bark. It is possible to become embedded within four to six weeks. It is better to loosen the wire a little too early than too late. Wiring a section of the tree several times one after the other will not damage it.

After wiring, the bonsai will need time to recover. Keep it out of direct sunlight. Spray it frequently and never repot at the same time.

Tree-shaping without the use of wires

There are other methods besides wiring for bending a branch downwards or upwards, or for bringing two branches closer together. Such methods need a bit more time and probably leave more to chance, but they are easier on the eye. In the examples shown below bits of string, loops of wire and other bits and pieces are used to bring about a change in shape to the tree.

With any of these methods still be sure to treat the tree gently. Cushion the spots where the wire or string is to be attached, either using a piece of rubber or PVC.

Pulling a branch downwards

1) Hang a stone weight on the branch to pull it downwards.

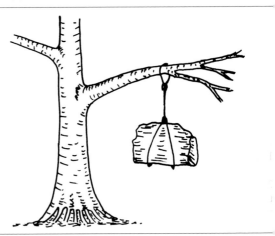

2) Tie the branch to the trunk with a piece of wire or
string.

3) Tie wires to the pot. They will act as a support for
individual bits of string being used to bend the
branch (or branches) downwards.

1) Use a piece of wood to bend the branches apart.

2) Bend branches towards one another and tie
together.

**Changing the
direction of growth
of branches**

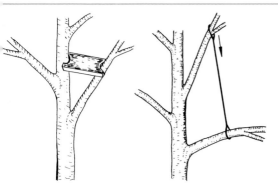

Suitable bonsai dishes The container you choose for your bonsai is just as important as the frame you choose for a picture. It needs to be carefully selected to complement the size, shape and colour of the tree.

Most containers are shallow pots in subdued colours which allow the tree to make its impact. Often their shape and colour acts as a counterbalance to the plant.

Old and valuable bonsai dishes from China.

The art of hand-made ceramic pots, like the art of bonsai itself, has a centuries-old tradition in China and Japan. In Europe valuable collections of these old and highly-prized pots have already been built up. Specialist bonsai shops stock a good variety of

A few examples of the pots currently on the market.

pots, some glazed, some unglazed, some tall, others shallow, some round, others oval or angular, but all have large drainage holes – so important in bonsai keeping. The more valuable bonsai you can get to see, the more confident you will feel about choosing the correct pot for your specimen. Nevertheless there are some rules of thumb which even experienced bonsai growers adhere to.

The *height* of the pot should not be less than the thickness of the trunk. The *length* of the pot can equal a third of the height of the tree. If you choose too small a pot, your tree will look cramped and will also not have enough support. A pot that is too big will detract from the overall effect of the tree – it is simply swamped by the pot.

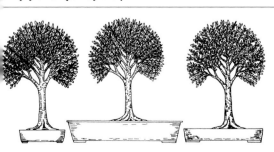

Pots that are too small (left), too big (centre) and just right.

Gardenia jasminoides, *approximately 35 years old and 55 cm (22 in) high. From the collection of Takeyama, Japan.*

Flowering trees and species that have light-green leaves harmonise best with light-coloured and glazed dishes. Dark foliage is best shown off in a dark-coloured container in a red, grey or brown colour.

Ficus retusa with round leaves, approximately 20 years old and 50 cm (20 in) high. From the collection of Pin Kewpaisal, Thailand.

Trees that grow upright look particularly attractive in shallow dishes. A pendulous style of tree looks better counterbalanced by a deep dish.

Glazed and unglazed containers are equally suitable for growing bonsai; just make sure the glaze is not continued on the inside.

Special features of Indoor Bonsai Arrangements

Creating a small indoor forest

Every keeper of indoor bonsai eventually decides to try to capture for himself the exotic effect of a tropical rain forest. It is a feature of bonsai cultivation that is easy to achieve provided that you possess a little skill and a good sense of proportion. Unusually, it demands no patience on the grower's behalf, as the forest is complete as soon as you have planted it, so you do not have to wait years to appreciate the effect. Of course you will always have the opportunity later of improving an individual tree's appearance, or of repotting one or two, or of swapping some altogether.

An indoor bonsai forest composed of Ficus benjamina. *Age range approximately 3–10 years, height 35 cm (14 in). Arranged by Henry Lorenz, Germany.*

The container used for an indoor bonsai forest should be very shallow, and oval or rectangular in shape. The standard size is 40 × 30 × 4 cm (16 × 12 × 1½ in).

In Japan bonsai specialists have drawn up various blueprints for planting an indoor forest, each artist of course laying down his own principles. Provided that a few basic guidelines are followed, however, even a beginner can create a really lovely forest, full of atmosphere, and without too much effort.

There should be at least five trees. Seven or nine, or even more, are better still. The uneven number of trees is important if the forest is to be made up of a small number of specimens. Arrange them into two groups, one a little larger and taller than the other.

Use young trees, two to six years old, for planting in your forest. It is less expensive in the first instance, and you will also be able to experience every development. Make the forest look even more interesting and true to nature by adding a few small ferns and other ground plants.

Do not plant a mixed forest, i.e. do not have different species of tree in the one tray. It might look very attractive but the living conditions and needs of the various trees would make looking after them very difficult. Choose instead plants of the same species but varying in height, thickness and age. Pick out the tree that is tallest and thickest and plant it first in the pot, as this will be the most important specimen in the whole arrangement. Do not put it right in the middle of the pot, but a little to one side. Now arrange the other trees either individually or as groups around your main tree. Specimens that have particularly well-formed branches on one side should be placed on the outside and smaller plants towards the back, thus helping to create the illusion of depth.

The exotic Weeping Fig (*Ficus benjamina*) is a favourite forest specimen which serves as a good example to show the phases of putting the arrangement together. Following this simple pattern, you will not find it difficult to implement your own ideas for making more imaginative and possibly larger forests.

Group planting

129

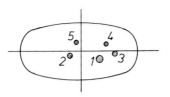

Make a sketch of your forest, as you imagine it, following the basic rules already described.

Get everything together that you will need.

Remove the trees from their pots, cutting off all unwanted branches and any leaves that are too big. Remove excess soil until only the main clump is left. Prune the roots by about a third and sort the plants according to size.

Plant the main tree (1) first, slightly off-centre. It should be the tree that is thickest and tallest. The next tree (2), slightly smaller, should be placed to the left of the main one and slightly towards the back. With these two specimens you have already determined the front and back of your arrangement.

Tree no. 3 should be placed to the right of the main tree, slightly towards the back. The gap between it and the main tree is less than that between the main tree and no. 2.

The fourth tree should be positioned between the main tree and no. 3, and towards the back.

The fifth and last tree should be placed to the right behind tree no. 2. Soil should now be added to the dish and then it should be watered thoroughly.

Serissa forest in windswept style. Approximately 25 years old and 35 cm (14 in) high.

You can apply this same arrangement or something similar to inclined trees, or even create a windswept forest. The only thing to remember is that all the trees must incline in the same direction, as in nature.

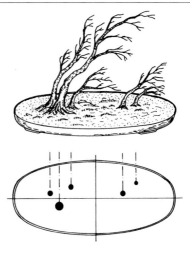

Sketch and planting plan for a windswept indoor forest.

An elm forest from the collection of Yin Chin Chang, Taiwan. Approximately 100 years old and 51 cm (20 in) high.

Caring for your indoor forest

Bonsai forests need the same sort of care routine as individual specimens of the same species. The forest arrangement makes a complete unit in itself – even the roots unite into a single entity.

After two years the forest will need repotting. By that time the trees will have formed a common root ball so you will be able to lift the entire arrangement from its pot and repot it. Do not forget to prune the roots.

Important points regarding a bonsai forest arrangement

Usually two tree groups need to be planted.
Vary the gaps between the trees.
Position the main tree a little off-centre.
No tree should be hidden from view.
Trees that are well formed on one side should be placed on the outside. You will need five, seven or nine trees of the same species, but varying in size, thickness and age (but all two to six years old).
Standard dish size required: 40 × 30 × 4 cm (16 × 12 × 1½ in).

135

Rock plantings

There are two basic types of rock planting, one of which, where the plant's roots run down over a rock into the soil in the pot, is particularly suitable for indoor bonsai species.

The long roots of this Carmona microphylla *have been trained over an old root rather than a rock. Approximately 18 years old and 30 cm (12 in) high.*

Plants with long, strong roots, such as many *Ficus* species, *Schefflera* and *Carmona*, are well suited for this interesting, if rather bizarre, bonsai arrangement. Ready-trained bonsai, as well as pot plants, bought or otherwise, are equally suitable for rock planting.

It is of course a simple job if you can find a plant whose roots are already long enough to train over the rock and down into the soil in the pot; but that will only happen on rare occasions. Most bonsai trees will have to be prepared in advance for a root-over-rock planting and this can take months.

To encourage the roots to grow, the tree should be planted in a plastic bucket or firm plastic bag. Whatever container is used for this, it should be at least as tall as the rock you have selected for your planting. The right soil to use for root growth is an equal parts mixture (50:50) of peat and sand, or you may prefer ready-made bonsai earth. In addition, the bucket or plastic bag will still need to have drainage holes.

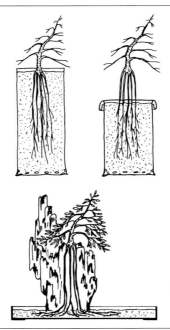

The plant container is trimmed further and further back to reveal a greater and greater amount of the root system.

Every six to eight weeks your plant container should be shortened by a couple of centimetres, so that each time a greater proportion of the roots will be left showing. With the bucket, cut it down a strip at a time; with the plastic bag, roll it back bit by bit, in each instance reducing the level of the soil to below the rim. The sections of root still buried beneath the soil will start to grow quicker and stronger in a downwards direction.

When there is only 5–8 cm (2–3 in) left of the container and the greater part of the root system is showing, it is time to transfer the plant to the pot you have selected.

Many bonsai keepers like to include the rock in the root growing stage. It is 'planted' in with the tree right from the beginning so the roots can be trained to grow in a particular direction.

So that the roots grow over the rock right from the start, the rock is planted in with the tree.

The impact of a rock planting is of course enhanced by the choice of rock or stone. Keep your eyes peeled when you are out for a walk and you may well find some attractive and unusual ones.

The rock

The size of the rock and its relation to the plant will set the mood for the scene you will end up creating. If you want to give the impression of distance, for example, put a small tree on a relatively large stone. You can really let your imagination run riot – after all, in nature almost anything is possible, every conceivable shape and proportion.

Small trees on a large rock create an impression of distance.

Large trees on a small rock make everything seem near enough to touch.

How to plant your prepared tree over the rock

Ficus benjamina *'Starlight' and other embellishments needed to make a bonsai arrangement.*

Carefully take the tree out of its container, loosening the soil from the roots with a piece of stick.

Alternatively, rinse the roots in water.

Remove any roots that are too thick or unappealing to the eye. Otherwise, do not prune any of the roots.

Place the plant on the rock and spread the roots out nicely and evenly in every direction.

Tie the rock in place with the wire you have already prepared, pushing it down far enough for the finely-branching fibrous roots to be covered with soil.

The tree is put in place and its roots spread out evenly all round.

The rock is fixed in place with wire and the roots covered with earth.

141

A very exotic and interesting effect can be created with rock plantings using tropical trees whose aerial roots are trained to run along the outside of the rock and down into the soil. The combination of roots and aerial roots lends a highly unusual charm to the whole arrangement.

After a rock planting has been set up it will need time to recover. Keep it out of direct sunlight and spray it frequently. Do not give any fertiliser for eight weeks, but from then on care for it exactly as you would any other indoor bonsai: add water and fertiliser to the soil and spray at regular intervals. With rock plantings the plant and rock form a single unit and should always be repotted together.

Sageretia *and* Carmona *planted on slate.*

Planting in crevices

The second basic type of rock planting is one where the plant is rooted on the rock itself and has no contact with the soil in the pot. This allows the rock to be placed on a tray containing water or sand to create the illusion of an island or mountain.

The bonsai trees themselves will grow in hollows and crevices in the rock, making it important that you find a suitable rock in the first place. The soil required is an equal parts mixture of peat and loam (50:50), plus some water, a layer 1–2 cm ($\frac{1}{2}$–$\frac{3}{4}$ in) deep being inserted into the selected hollows on the rock. Now add your plants, securing them with wire that has previously been stuck to the rock with some bonded adhesive. Cover the roots with some more of the soil mixture. Any roots that you cannot fit into the hollow should be spread out on the adjoining rock, trimmed slightly, then smeared with more soil. Next come the ground plants. Press them carefully into the loam-peat mixture and secure in place with hairpin-shaped clips. The plants you choose as ground cover must be capable of spreading quickly over the surface of the soil to help prevent any soil being washed away when the plant is watered. Moss, for example, only grows out of doors, so for indoor plantings it is better to use evergreen creepers such as *Soleirolia*, *Pilea microphylla*, *Selaginella* or *Nertera*.

Evergreen plants that thrive indoors and are therefore suitable as ground cover for indoor bonsai arrangements.

Keep the ground plants short – if they do grow too tall, trim them back. Rock plantings need to be sprayed frequently to stop them drying out. Water carefully to prevent soil from being washed away. Do not feed for eight weeks and then give only a small amount of liquid fertiliser. Periodically replace any soil that has been washed away.

Important points regarding rock plantings

There are two basic types of rock planting.

1) Root over rock and down into soil in dish
To prepare your plant you will need the following.

A plastic bucket or plastic bag.
An equal parts mixture (50:50) of peat and sand or bonsai earth.
A rock or stone which you should be able to find when out walking.
Patience – it may take a year or more for the tree to grow sufficiently long roots.
For planting the roots must be long enough for the ends to reach the bonsai earth in the pot. To grow the roots put the tree in a plastic container with a light soil (and do not forget your drainage holes).

For planting you will need the following.

A plant with long, strong roots.
A rock or stone.
A bonsai pot that complements the stone.
Bonsai soil.
A piece of stick.

A rock planting should not be given fertiliser for eight weeks, but should be sprayed frequently. Always water onto the bonsai earth.

2) Plant rooted on the rock itself
The rock you choose will need to have well-defined hollows. It may be placed in a pot containing water or sand. Fill the hollows with a layer of peat/loam soil mixture (50:50) then add the plants. Any roots that cannot be fitted into the hollow should be spread out on the adjoining rock. Trim back the longest root tips but do not cut off an entire root. Add more of the peat/loam mixture to the hollow,

Ficus natalensis, *approximately 18 years old and 50 cm (20 in) high. From the collection of Bob Richards, South Africa.*

then proceed with your ground cover plants. Your tree will be fixed in place with wire and your ground plants with hairpin-shaped clips. Carefully spray your arrangement once finished but do not add fertiliser for eight weeks.

The art of creating a natural-looking landscape in the smallest of spaces probably originated in China; but in Japan too, saikei – a small landscape on a tray – has its own tradition. The world-renowned Japanese gardens provided the inspiration, and even today there is a very well-known school in Tokyo that specialises in teaching the art of saikei.

Saikei is made up of natural elements, plants, soil, rocks and sand – materials that you can collect yourself. No other form of bonsai gives your imagination so much room for experiment.

As with the indoor forest, experienced bonsai people always advise against mixing different species of tree on one tray; instead, have trees of the same species but of varying sizes. Not only is it easier to care for, but your landscape will hang together better. The same does not apply to the ground cover plants, however. You can mix a wide variety of these together if you wish.

If children are involved in creating your landscape, or if you simply like the idea, you can include a few figures, model bridges or houses in your design. True saikei, however, are composed entirely of natural elements.

Saikei – a miniature landscape for indoors

(Opposite) Close-up of a Chinese miniature landscape. Arrangement by Yu Yat Sham, Hong Kong.

To set up your indoor bonsai landscape follow the guidelines given for repotting; for the arrangement use similar ideas to the indoor forest. The first step is to gather together everything you need. As with the forest it is best to use young, good quality plants, between one and three years old.

The character of your landscape will to a large extent be determined by the rocks and stones you use. Just by the shape of your rocks, their size in relation to the trees, even where you place them in the pot, you can create different effects – a hilly or mountainous landscape, an island or a peninsula. A main rock that is bigger and taller than your largest plant, for example, will loom like a chalky cliff in your landscape.

An indoor bonsai landscape composed of Carmona microphylla.

The type of pot you should use for a landscape bonsai is the same as for an indoor forest – shallow, and oval or rectangular in shape. A very large pot will make your landscape look more dramatic. Drainage holes covered with plastic mesh should not be forgotten.

148

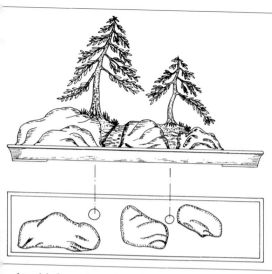

Sketch showing a miniature landscape.

As with forest bonsai, make a rough sketch of how you imagine your finished landscape will look.

For all saikei that start life as an idea that is later to be realised in a pot there is one guiding principle: start with your main tree and the rock that is to go with it. If you wish these major elements to be linked optically, both will have to be placed on the central axis of the pot. If the main intention, however, is to create the illusion of depth, the rock should be placed slightly towards the back.

Once you have your rocks and trees just where you want them, fill the pot with bonsai earth, remembering that it too is part of the design of your landscape, and requires more than just being smoothed over. The way the soil rises and falls all adds to the structure and character of your scene. Lastly, you will need to plant some grasses, evergreen creepers or, maybe, some small ferns. You can ring the changes with your ground cover plants as much as you like, but it should be remembered that mosses are not very suitable for indoor landscapes as they only flourish out in the open.

The examples shown on the following pages will, I hope, excite your imagination and give you an idea of how varied and attractive saikei arrangements can be.

Indoor landscapes make no special demands as far as their care is concerned. For a few weeks after it has been set up, you should be particularly careful with saikei – do not give any fertiliser and keep it out of direct sunlight, but make sure that it gets plenty of light all the same!

Important points regarding landscape bonsai

You will need the following:

A shallow, oval or rectangular pot.
Plastic mesh to cover the drainage holes.
Gravel, in various, but naturally-occurring colours.

Bonsai soil.
Young (one to three years old) plants, all of the same species.
Rocks – at least one large one and several small ones.
Ground plants (grasses, ferns, *Selaginella*).
A lot of imagination.

Make a sketch to show where all the elements of the landscape are to be placed. Start with the main tree and the rock that is to go with it. Follow the planting instructions given for individual indoor bonsai and indoor forests.

After completing the landscape do not feed it for a few weeks, but stand it in a bright spot, out of direct sunlight.

Saikei made up of Chaemacyparis pisifera Nana, *from the collection of Toshio Kawamoto, Japan.*

An indoor landscape made up of a Ficus, *grasses and* Selaginella.

Creating your Own Indoor Bonsai

About 40 per cent of the earth's surface is covered with tropical rain forest, and it is there that more than 10,000 different species of tree grow. Added to this is a huge variety of subtropical plants with beautiful and spectacular blooms. So, theoretically, if you want to cultivate your own indoor bonsai the choice is unlimited. In reality, however, it is limited to those plants whose seeds can be bought or collected and those from which cuttings can be obtained. Every year, however, the bonsai trade is able to offer a greater selection.

Just take a look at the old familiar pot plants that are available – the full-sized versions are very often stately trees that grow in tropical and subtropical regions – and you will get a good indication of the variety of plants that can be trained as bonsai. Of course, not all are as suitable for training as others. For further information turn to pages 32–87 and 191–9.

Collecting plants

Many old and highly-prized bonsai with lovely shapes have often been found originally by their owners perhaps while they were out walking in some mountains or among some rocks. Having been located, the plant would have been dug up and its training carried out back at the owner's home. Of course most of the plants that grow in temperate climes are not suitable for keeping indoors. Those who live reasonably close to where the plants mentioned in this book are indigenous may be tempted to collect fine natural specimens themselves; however it is imperative that you are aware of the law in that country as it applies to the taking of wild plants, and almost certainly the permission of the owner of the land should be sought. If you find you can dig up an interesting and suitable specimen without breaking the law or upsetting the land-owner then try to do so during the least active growing season so that you can give the tree a chance to survive. Before digging up any specimen cut off any small, unimportant branches to reduce the evaporation surface of the tree.

Go as deep as you can to dig the plant out so that you retain as much of the root area as possible, as well as surrounding soil. Remember above all that the finely-branching fibrous roots are especially important for the intake of food.

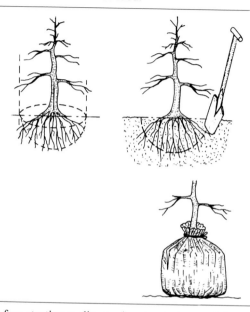

Before digging up any tree (in the correct manner!) ask the owner (e.g. the local authority) for permission.

Before starting to dig, mark out a circle round the trunk roughly the same size in diameter as the crown of the tree. Cut down into the earth along this line, then take the tree out very carefully, leaving as much of the soil attached as possible.

The best time of year to go collecting is the beginning of spring, just before growth activity restarts. It can nevertheless be said that many a plant has been brought back for bonsai training from a summer holiday and has still been turned into a lovely indoor specimen. The important thing is to pack the plant straight away into a lot of wet newspaper or moss and then place the whole plant inside a plastic bag. Once you get home again transfer the specimen immediately to a plant pot, shield it from the sun and make sure that the surrounding humidity level is high. It is an excellent idea to put a see-through plastic bag punched with holes over your plant for four to six weeks to prevent water loss through evaporation. After about a year, once the first root pruning has taken place, you will be able to transfer your tree to a bonsai pot.

Important points regarding specimen collection

You will need the following.

A small spade.
A pair of bonsai scissors.
A good supply of wet newspaper and plastic bags.

Dig down deep enough so that you do not rip out the fine fibrous roots. With older plants mark out a circle round the plant, roughly the same size in diameter as the crown of the tree, then cut along this line.

Spring and autumn are the best times of year to go collecting. Keep your specimen well moistened on the journey home. After a year being kept in a plant pot, prune the roots, then transfer it to a bonsai pot.

The bonsai enthusiast would probably like nothing better than to witness the development of an attractive, interestingly-shaped tree from a single seed. In this connection, however, there is one common myth I would like to dispel immediately: there are no such things as bonsai seeds. Whatever is written on packets of so-called 'bonsai seeds', all it means is that the plant is suitable for bonsai training. An indoor bonsai produced from seed is really a houseplant that has been grown and at a later date shaped into a bonsai. (For suppliers, see Appendix.) Every box contains precise instructions for sowing the seeds. Apart from buying seeds or collecting them on holiday along the Mediterranean and all countries south, the more resourceful hunter may like to take a look in his local delicatessen. Some specimens of great charm can be grown from avocados, pomegranates, pistachios, citrus fruits and such like.

Indoor bonsai from seeds

Every old, gnarled bonsai brimful of character originally developed from a single seed; but between the collection or purchase of the seed and its becoming a miniature tree, more properly called a bonsai, several years will have passed. The same is true of indoor bonsai even though most of them grow more quickly than outdoor species.

Patience is what is needed

Different species of seed will differ in the length of time that they will remain capable of germination. With some it will be only a matter of a few days; with others it might last years. Types that age quickly should be sown immediately or kept buried in damp sand until required for sowing. Other types of seed are still not capable of germination even when the fruit ripens. They must first be stratified, which means they must be kept for several months at a cool but frost-free temperature, 2–8°C (36–46°F), to bring them to maturity.

Try your luck and sow any seeds that you think might turn into nice pot plants – lemon pips, mandarins etc. – then wait. Some will start to sprout instantly, some perhaps after a year, some never, but whatever the case it is always worth having a go.

Indoor bonsai from fruits

Name of Fruit	Name of Plant
Carambola	*Averrhoa carambola*
Cherimoya	*Annona cherimola*
Citrus	*Citrus* Lemon
	Citrus aurantifolia
	Citrus sinensis
Durian	*Durio zibethinus*
Custard apple	*Annona muricada*
Pomegranate	*Punica granatum*
Guava	*Psidium guajaba*
Carob bean	*Ceratonia siliqua*
Surinam cherry	*Eugenia uniflora*
Loquat	*Eribotrya japonica*
Lychee	*Litchi chinensis*
Cassia	*Cassia fistula*
Pistachio	*Pistacia*
Burdock-like nephelium	*Nephelium lappaceum*
Sapodilla	*Acharas zapota*
Tamarillo	*Cyphomandra betacea*

Before sowing

Many types of seed must be made to swell first of all. To do this, simply put them in water and leave them there for 24 hours, remembering that hard seeds should be scored first with a file. Seeds that are ready for germination will absorb enough water to make them sink to the bottom of the container, whereas infertile ones will stay floating on the surface. Sow the fertile seeds while still moist – never allow them to dry out again after soaking in water.

Sowing the seeds

The seedling is surrounded with nutrient tissue so only requires 'poor' soil. It should not contain any fertiliser, or very little, and should be free of possible disease carriers or contamination. A peat-sand mixture is ideal (the bigger the seeds the more coarse-grained the soil), various proprietary brands being readily available. You may of course prefer to mix your own soil, in which case it should be in the ratio one part peat to one part sand. Plastic seed trays, 8–10 cm (3–4 in) in depth, are best for sowing,

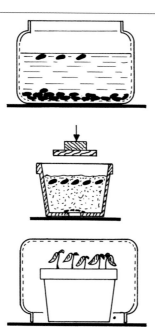

How to sow seeds.

although you can use bonsai pots or any kind of
plastic pot. It is only important that whatever you
use has drainage holes covered with plastic mesh to
stop soil trickling out. Jiffy pots are good for sowing
single seeds.

Fill the pot with soil up to 3 cm (1 in) below the
rim, then smooth it over with a piece of wood. Now
you are ready to sow your seeds. Place large seeds
exactly where you want them; scatter smaller and
finer ones, but try to keep the spread even. Press the
larger seeds gently into the soil and cover with a thin
layer of sieved soil, about as deep as the thickness of
the seed. Very fine seeds do not need a covering of
soil; simply press them in very gently. To keep your
seedlings healthy once they start developing, use
captan powder.

Watering seeds

Keep the seed trays out of direct sunlight but make sure that the soil always remains moist – but not wet! To stop the seeds bunching together during watering, it is better to use a fine spray or diffuser. Alternatively, you could stand the tray for about five minutes in some water that reaches three-quarters of the way up the pot. Choose a site that has a nice even temperature, 18–22°C (64–72°F).

As soon as the first four or five leaflets appear, the young plants should be transplanted or placed in individual pots. A month afterwards at the earliest add some fertiliser for the first time. An organic liquid fertiliser is best, but only ever use half the prescribed amount, at the most.

Once the seedlings are 8–12 cm (3–5 in) tall you can start to alter the growth pattern. By cutting away the top of the main shoot, for example, the seedling will develop new, lateral shoots and it will start to branch.

Once your tree is 15–20 cm (6–8 in) tall and has hardened a little, you can start bonsai-training. It goes without saying that you should choose the most promising specimens for this.

*Murraya paniculata
grown from seed.*

You will need the following.

Seeds.
A plastic container, about 10 cm (4 in) in depth,
with drainage holes, a bonsai dish or jiffy pots (for
owing single seeds).
Moist sand for stratification, if necessary.
Soil: a peat-sand mixture.
A piece of wood.
A sieve.

Fill the container with the soil up to 3 cm (1 in)
below the rim, add the seeds, then sprinkle with a
thin layer of sieved soil. (Very fine seeds do not need
a soil covering.)

Keep the seed trays moist at all times. Transfer the
young plants to individual pots and add some
fertiliser after three months at the earliest.

**Important points
regarding indoor
bonsai from seeds**

**Creating a bonsai
from a seedling**

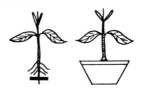

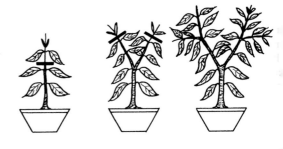

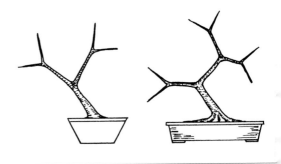

Cuttings are shoots or young branches that are nipped off the parent plant. If placed in soil or water, roots will develop and the cuttings will turn into self-sustaining plants. Many cuttings develop roots very easily, some have a bit more difficulty, but nearly all plants can be propagated by the cuttings method.

If you like, you can of course use any off-cuts from your bonsai tree during training to grow new trees. You need only make sure that you carry out the pruning correctly to produce the right sort of cuttings (see below).

Indoor bonsai from cuttings

How your cuttings should look.

The cutting should be about 10–20 cm (4–8 in) long and slightly woody, i.e. not too soft.

Snip the cutting off directly below a leaf node using a sharp knife or a pair of bonsai scissors. If the tip of the shoot is very soft, trim it a little.

Remove any leaves from the end that is to be stuck into the soil, to leave about 3 cm (1 in) clear.

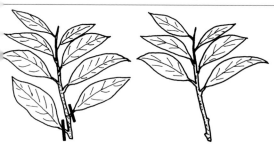

Giving bonsai treatment to a seedling.

Next dip the end in some rooting powder, although this is not vital. Rooting powders are readily available from shops, their function being to encourage the development of roots. The really important thing to remember is to keep the time between taking the cutting from the parent plant and placing it in the soil as short as possible, to prevent wilting.

The exceptions to this rule are the succulents (e.g. Jade plants). The cut ends must be allowed to dry before planting in soil, so let them lie around for about 14 days. Only then can they be put in some *dry* soil. Only water after the first fine, white roots have formed.

Flowerpots, seed trays, bonsai pots or wooden boxes are all suitable as plant containers. Do not forget, however, that they should all have drainage holes covered with plastic mesh. Fill your pot with an equal parts mixture of peat and sand, pressing it down lightly with a bit of wood. Now plant the cuttings about 2–3 cm (1 in) down into the soil, leaving enough space between each cutting to stop them touching.

Next water thoroughly, and either cover your pot with a see-through plastic bag or invert a glass cucumber frame over it to make a small propagator.

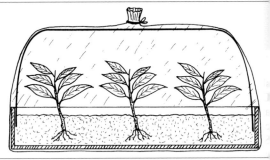

Keep the soil moist at all times and spray the cuttings frequently.

For the first three months keep your mini-glasshouse somewhere bright, but out of direct sunlight.

Cuttings taken from tropical plants need to be kept in a warm site, 18–24°C (64–75°F); cold-house cuttings a little cooler. After four to eight weeks, depending on species, when the first roots have formed, you can start to add a small amount of fertiliser and also begin to accustom your plants to the air (i.e. take the cover off). Once a nice lot of roots have developed the specimens should be transferred to individual pots 6–8 cm (2½–3 in) high. Trim any overlong root tips at the same time as this will encourage a more even, compact root ball.

A Sageretia *cutting well enough rooted for planting.*

Many houseplants provide cuttings that can simply be placed in water for enough roots to grow. Do not use narrow-necked bottles for this, however, as you might damage the roots when you take the cutting out. Ordinary drinking glasses are suitable. Stand glasses containing cold-house specimens on a window ledge away from a heat source; tropical varieties on a window ledge over a radiator. Using glass containers has the added advantage of letting you see how many roots have formed. Once there are enough, transfer your plant immediately to an individual pot.

Many people do not start shaping their tree for about a year, but there is nothing to stop you trimming the new shoots a little right from the beginning.

New shoots are trimmed from the start. The plant will start to branch out.

Ficus neriifolia *grown from cuttings: 2 years (left), 4 years (centre) and 15 years old.*

Important points regarding indoor bonsai from cuttings

You will need the following.

A sharp knife or a pair of bonsai scissors.

Then either:
Any sort of plant container with covered drainage hole
An equal parts peat-sand soil mixture (50:50).
A plastic bag or glass cucumber frame to make a propagator.

Or: A glass container with water in it.

Many plants that can be kept indoors are suitable for propagation using cuttings at any time of the year, but it is best carried out between mid-spring and early summer. Once sufficient roots have formed each plant should be planted in its own pot, 6–8 cm (2½–3 in) high, containing indoor bonsai earth. Give fertiliser after about three to four weeks.

Air-layering

Cuttings taken from branches that have grown as thick as your fingers stand little if any chance of 'taking'. They have to be rooted by a technique known as air-layering, whereby the roots of the new plant develop while it is still attached to the parent plant. The young plant is removed from the trunk of the original tree only when it is self-supporting, i.e. when enough roots have formed for it to be able to feed itself. In the meantime bonsai-training can be started – while the branch is developing roots attached to the parent plant, you can prune it and even wire it, if necessary. It is a method that can produce a lovely mature-looking specimen fairly quickly. One example is the Weeping Fig shown in the picture below, which had been kept for some time in a living room before being air-layered.

Ficus benjamina *before and after air-layering.*

Air-layering can be carried out at any time of year, although roots will develop more quickly during the main growing season.

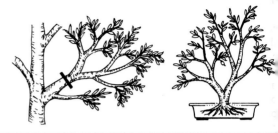

From a nicely-shaped branch can emerge a nicely-shaped tree.

Select a particularly attractive branch from your pot plant, as this will form the trunk of your future bonsai specimen. Choose one not bigger than 5–20 mm ($\frac{1}{10}$–$\frac{3}{4}$ in) in diameter, otherwise it can take a very long time for roots to form.

Make a tongue-shaped slit, 2 cm ($\frac{3}{4}$ in) long, going from bottom to top, on both sides of the selected branch where you want roots to develop. Dab some hormone rooting powder onto the incision.

Put a small stone, or a piece of moss or peat, into the slit to prevent the wound from closing again.

Fix a piece of polythene underneath the wound and fill it with moist peat or sphagnum moss. Use a see-through polythene so that you can see the roots forming.

Take the polythene upwards and tie the end with a rubber band or piece of string. The seal should be good enough to stop much water loss through evaporation.

Several weeks may go by before any new roots appear. During this time keep testing that the peat or moss is still moist, and if necessary, add a bit more water to the polythene sleeve from above.

Depending on the species of plant, enough new roots will have formed after six to eight weeks for the new tree to live independently. Now the branch can be separated from its parent plant by cutting it off beneath the original point of incision. Plant it immediately in a pot, without removing the moss or peat, or put it straight away into a suitable bonsai pot.

Air-layering, using the tongue-shaped slit method.

Apart from the tongue-shaped slit method, there are two other types of air-layering techniques: constriction using wire; and the peeling away of a strip of bark about 1 cm ($\frac{1}{2}$ in) wide from the selected branch.

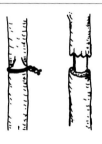

Two alternative air-layering techniques.

The same principle applies to plants that have been obtained by the air-layering technique as to any plants: allow the plant to become well rooted in its new pot before continuing with the bonsai training.

Important points regarding air-layering

You will need the following.

A sharp knife.
Peat, sphagnum moss.
See-through plastic film and a bit of string or a rubber band.

Any branch chosen for air-layering must be selected carefully as it will eventually form the trunk of your bonsai.

Incisions are made on both sides of the selected branch. Refer to diagrams.

Apply a plastic sleeve containing peat around the incision. Keep the peat moist at all times. Then wait. Only remove the sleeve when a good quantity of root is showing through the peat. When you take it off make sure that the ball of peat does not disintegrate.

Air-layering takes four to eight weeks or longer for results to show. Once enough roots have formed, plant in a pot.

The first step towards an indoor bonsai

Whether you have cultivated a young plant yourself, found one growing in the wild, or bought one, or even if your intention is to train a mature pot plant as a bonsai, taking the first step towards shaping that bonsai is always eagerly anticipated. Your carefully selected specimen is going to experience its first root pruning, it is going to be planted in a carefully chosen bonsai pot, and its basic shape is about to be determined. Turn to the sections entitled 'Repotting and Root Pruning' and 'Shaping Your Indoor Bonsai' for step-by-step instructions and look through the examples on the following pages for some ideas. Enjoy yourself!

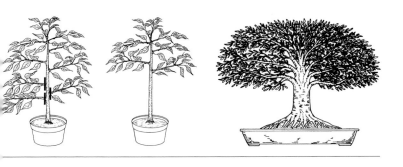

Punica granatum
bent downwards and fixed firmly in place. After three months it will have developed a cascading style.

Cissus antarctica
trained in the literati style.

Ficus benjamina
'Starlight'.

Myrtus communis,
*approximately two
years old and 8 cm
(3 in) high. Trained
by Michael Veith,
Germany.*

171

Ficus benjamina,
*together with its pot,
is first laid
horizontally in the
soil. After about eight
weeks the branches
will be growing
upwards, at which
point the ball of earth
can be cut off and the
resulting raft form
planted in a bonsai
pot.*

Ficus benjamina –
*three specimens
woven into a twisting
trunk.*

172

A two-year-old
Schefflera arboricola
– its first pruning.

An eight-year-old
Schefflera arboricola
trained in an umbrella style.

173

A six-year-old Myrtus communis, *seen here as a pot plant. Within this triple-trunked specimen there lie informal upright and slanting styles.*

Sketch showing one of the possibilities, a slightly slanting style. The photos show the plant trained as a windswept bonsai.

Myrtus communis,
*wired into a
windswept style.*

*The same specimen
one year later.*

175

Ficus benjamina *as a pot plant.*

The same Ficus *trained in a weeping willow style, after leaf pruning, and six months later.*

Grevillea robusta
*trained into a curved
informal upright
style.*

Ficus benjamina
*trained into a
spherical style.*

Indoor Bonsai from Pot Plants

The Right Tool

If you have already got some experience of bonsai and are fully conversant with the care and training of miniature trees out of doors, you are bound to be well equipped for managing indoor species. If you have only just taken up the hobby, however, it is well worth buying the most essential tools right from the start. You will make everything much easier for yourself and you will get more enjoyment from your hobby.

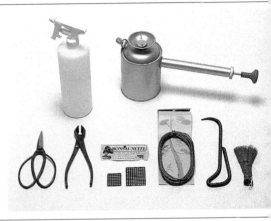

Tools needed right from the start

1) A plant spray (metal or plastic).
2) Bonsai scissors for cutting shoots, twigs, thin branches and roots.
3) Concave-cutting pliers, used for cutting off branches very close to the trunk in such a way that the wound heals quickly and with minimum scarring.
4) Plastic mesh for covering drainage holes.
5) Anodised aluminium wire in various thicknesses.
6) A hook for untangling matted roots when repotting. A stick will do the same job.
7) A bonsai brush for cleaning and smoothing the surface of the soil.

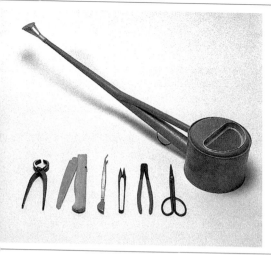

1) Pliers for cutting thick roots.

2) A bonsai saw for thick branches.

3) Bonsai tweezers for pinching out young shoots, withered leaves and aphids etc.

4) Leaf cutters.

5) Wire cutters so shaped that you can snip off the wire on the plant without damaging the bark.

6) A slender pair of bonsai scissors for cutting fine shoots and thinning out the crown.

7) Watering can with a fine spray nozzle.

Do not forget that your tools need looking after. Clean them regularly and oil them every so often.

Tools to acquire gradually

Mini Indoor Bonsai

In recent years the Japanese in particular seem to have developed a passion for really tiny bonsai. Mini bonsai for indoors and out are 8–15 cm (3–6 in) tall and still retain the shape of full-grown plants or even of trees. The pots they are coming in are miniature versions of the larger bonsai pots, coming in a great variety of shapes and colours but often no bigger than a thimble.

The indoor varieties of mini bonsai are particularly attractive and decorative, either by themselves or several placed together on a tray filled with sand or gravel.

How do you obtain a mini indoor bonsai?

As with the larger forms of indoor bonsai you can quite easily cultivate the mini versions yourself from seeds or from cuttings taken from pot plants or other indoor bonsai. The smaller the leaves on your plant the more pleasing the proportions on your eventual mini specimen. Once you are well attuned to bonsai you will automatically select cuttings that already have an interesting shape and will develop an attractive appearance relatively quickly. 'Attractive', as far as mini bonsai are concerned, still means creating a natural and harmonious effect.

A mini indoor bonsai grown from a plant cutting does not warrant the name for at least three years. Training is simple, as the goal you want to achieve is clear: the plant as a whole and its individual leaves should be kept as small as possible. So right from the start you should keep pinching out all new shoots – leaving one or two leaves only – at the same time removing any big leaves. Gradually your cutting will start developing its own unique shape.

Caring for mini bonsai

In essence the same rules apply as for every other kind of indoor bonsai. What you need to remember is that a mini bonsai often has only two or three teaspoonfuls of soil from which to obtain its nutrition. For that reason you will have to water it more often, repot it more frequently and add fertiliser more carefully.

As I would describe watering mini bonsai more as a test of patience, I think it is more sensible to immerse the tiny pots in water. Do it at least once a day, leaving them underwater until no more bubbles can be seen rising to the surface. It is also a good idea to stand mini bonsai on a tray filled with sand or gravel that is kept moist at all times – never leave standing in water, however!

Repot about once a year, at the same time pruning the roots by about a third. The soil mixture you use is the same as for all bonsai, but finer. Do not add fertiliser for four to six weeks after repotting.

During the growing season feed your plant once a week using a liquid fertiliser but in a weaker solution. Always add to the moistened soil. If your pot is very small it is wiser to inject the fertiliser in from below through the drainage hole.

Important points regarding the care and training of mini indoor bonsai

They are easy to cultivate from seeds or cuttings. Right from the start cut off all new shoots (leaving one or two only) and big leaves.

Mini bonsai need to be watered more often, repotted more frequently and fed more carefully.

A tray filled with sand or gravel that is kept moist makes an attractive container for your mini pots and also makes them easier to care for.

Immersion is preferable to watering, and injection of fertiliser through a drainage hole is also a good idea.

Ficus benjamina *as a mini indoor bonsai.*

Hydroculture

Plants find nourishment from water and the mineral substances dissolved in it. In traditional pot plant cultivation they are planted in soil which provides not only support but also acts as a water and nutrient store.

In hydroculture plants are supported not by soil but by a structurally stable, porous substratum. They are rooted in water and 'automatically' provided with nutrients.

More and more hobbists are being attracted to hydroculture. No doubt this is partly explained by the fact that it makes caring for your plants easier as it is almost impossible to make any mistakes with watering and feeding. It also puts an end to the problem of what to do with your plants in the holidays. We will have to accustom ourselves to the idea of indoor bonsai grown by hydroculture before we proceed any further. They certainly look different to classical indoor bonsai in which the soil and bonsai dish play such an important part in the overall impression created by the miniature tree. Even gravel, however, can be arranged in an attractive way, and there are already quite a few different types of hydro-container on the market, most of which are suitable for bonsai.

The first time you try hydroculture, use cuttings that have been rooted in water. You will also find that young trees which grow vigorously will easily transfer to hydroculture.

Read as much as you can about hydroculture before getting to work.

Many bonsai enthusiasts find that they can take quite readily to hydroculture itself, but that they cannot abide the deep containers that need to be used. If you follow the method given below you will not have to abandon attractive bonsai pots, yet you can still switch your plants to the hydroculture system.

Remove the plant from its pot, rinse the roots in luke-warm water, removing all traces of soil. Even tiny bits of soil will increase the likelihood of bacterial decay.

Prune the roots back hard (by at least a third).

Place the plant in a bonsai pot and fill it with gravel (bits of broken clay, grain size 2–4 mm). Cover drainage holes with plastic mesh. Rinse the gravel in water and add to the pot while moist.

Stand the newly-potted bonsai on a watertight tray which has already been filled nearly up to the edge with the same gravel. Large, shallow trays with sides about 2–4 cm ($\frac{3}{4}$–$1\frac{1}{2}$ in) high are particularly attractive.

Jacaranda mimosifolia *(left)*, Pyracantha coccinea *(centre) and* Sageretia theezans *given hydroculture treatment.*

On the first occasion fill the tray completely with luke-warm tap water. When all but 1 cm ($\frac{1}{2}$ in) of the water has been used up, fill the tray again right to the top. After being transferred to the gravel-filled pot, your bonsai will be more sensitive than normal, so it is best to cover it with a see-through plastic bag for a fortnight or so. Once the two weeks have elapsed and new roots have formed, you can sprinkle on some hydro fertiliser.

If your aim is to make watering easier, at the same time avoiding making any mistakes with it, yet so far you have remained thoroughly unimpressed by hydroculture, you could use a soilless compost. Several bonsai hobbyists have already started to use this new material as a soil replacement, although it is not widely available. When they repot their tree, they put it, together with its ball of earth, in some of this material, instead of in new soil. It is made of porous clay granules, red-brown in colour, which both absorb water readily and release it again. It creates, in effect, a water reservoir, which can solve the main problems of watering, as the plant is always able to take as much moisture from the material as it needs.

In general, you should give the granules a good soak with a spray every eight days, or immerse the plant. If it is very hot in the summer water more frequently – about every three days. It is absolutely imperative to add water if ever the dark brown-red colour of the granules changes to something paler. Any excess water will run off through the drainage holes.

The porous clay material also ensures good air circulation around the roots. In addition, use a long-lasting plant food, and you can be certain that the plant will be well nourished at all times.

The use of soilless compost also makes it possible to have some ground-cover plants, something which makes this method more appealing to bonsai growers than hydroculture. If you want to gain some experience of this new material try it out on a young plant.

Buying Indoor Bonsai

Most bonsai hobbyists start off with a tree that has already been trained and subsequently add to their collection by buying other specimens and creating their own. Every year the trade is able to offer a more varied and interesting choice of indoor species. Whether the tree you are buying is young or old, whether you are buying it as a present or making yourself a present of one, you should always make certain that the plant is a healthy one, with well-established roots. To experienced bonsai growers an important sign of quality is that the tree has a good network of roots spreading throughout the ball of earth.

Any bonsai nurseryman will always be willing to show you the root system if asked. The plant will be lifted very carefully from its pot. It is of good quality if you can see that the ball of earth is firm with a nice spread of roots, the fine tips of which should be visible towards the outside edge (these are white in the growing season). The only exception to this rule is if you are buying a plant that has just been repotted.

What determines value

In bonsai-keeping age is often over-valued. Of course an older tree of some beauty is going to cost more than a young one that is merely pleasant-looking. Nevertheless, for the very reason that indoor bonsai-keeping is a relatively new hobby, the main point is the beauty of the plant, that it is well proportioned and has a well-balanced shape. So, when buying a specimen do not be blinded by how many years old it is, but be guided by your feeling for beauty and harmony – after all, a bonsai pot cannot make an indoor bonsai out of a pot plant.

You can train your eye to know what to look for in a bonsai by looking at pictures of good-quality ones and by going to exhibitions.

Bonsai experts are always being asked what are the objective criteria for judging the value of miniature trees. If it is possible to argue that there are any general hallmarks of beauty regarding indoor bonsai, I would opt for the following six.

1) A healthy, vigorous appearance.
2) A well-defined shape (see section entitled 'Shaping your Indoor Bonsai').
3) A trunk that tapers evenly towards the top.
4) Branches that taper towards the outside and which get finer and finer towards the crown.
5) Roots which spread out evenly on all sides from the bottom of the trunk but which do not cross.
6) Leaves in proportion to the tree, but of course not to scale, which are also strong and healthy-looking.

A properly-executed cut and well-healed scar.

Many collectors also want to know if visible cuts devalue a bonsai. The answer is no. If a cut is carried out properly using concave-cutting scissors and is kept clean, it will heal nicely and add character to the tree without diminishing its beauty.

The cost of indoor bonsai

Young plants, between one and three years old, that you will have to train as indoor bonsai, can be bought for between £2 and £5. A really beautiful indoor bonsai, always complete with pot, costs more than £40; and for a prize specimen you can often expect to pay £300–£1000. Just consider these sums of money for a moment, then think about technological products that are mass-produced in a matter of minutes – they often cost many times more than a bonsai. Keep in mind that a trained bonsai is often someone's life's work and as such represents a one-off piece of art. It bears testimony to many years' hard work, patience and devotion on the part of the artist.

Ficus retusa from the collection of Lian Lin. Approximately 60 years old and 55 cm (22 in) high.

Qualities of a prize specimen

To be considered a prize specimen, an indoor bonsai has to have an exceptionally beautiful growth pattern and be at least 15 years old. As the art of indoor bonsai does not have a tradition anywhere near as long as that of outdoor bonsai, however, prize indoor specimens are still very much a rarity even today. Anyone who owns one can therefore be justifiably proud of it.

Many towns have specialist bonsai retailers or garden centre outlets supplied by them. Only a bonsai dealer, however, is likely to be able to give you the necessary advice on care. Being a member of a bonsai club can be invaluable for picking up knowledge and advice quickly. The Federation of British Bonsai Societies maintains a register of such clubs in the UK, and their annually updated guide may be obtained from the Secretary, 52 Ashburn Road, Heaton Norris, Stockport, Cheshire SK4 2PU.

The best place to buy

You can tell a good specialist shop by the advice given. Examine the ball of soil before buying any plant. It should have a good spread of roots.

Age is only one factor when considering value. Especially with indoor species, form and shape are at least as important. An objective price comparison is difficult. Every indoor specimen is different. For ideas and advice I would recommend your local bonsai society (address given in Appendix).

Important points regarding the purchase of indoor bonsai

Ficus retusa,
*approximately 60
years old and 75 cm
(30 in) high.*

Tropical and Subtropical Plants Suitable for Training as Indoor Bonsai

All the species of plant in the following list have already been trained successfully as bonsai. Many of them have been described mainly in American, Indian and Chinese specialist bonsai books.

Occurring naturally in their subtropical and tropical homelands as outdoor plants, they are suitable as indoor bonsai in more temperate climates.

In the main the list includes trees and shrubs that can be bought as pot plants either from flower shops or garden centres or that you can find around the holiday areas of the Mediterranean. You may not always find the exact species described, but plants of the same genus have very similar requirements in the way of care. There may also be a botanical garden nearby that can provide cuttings. Many indoor specimens are also available through retail bonsai outlets, and every year the variety on offer increases.

Acacia baileyana
Acacia, 'Mimosa'

Subtropical and tropical trees with a pleasant growth pattern, small pinnate leaves and golden-yellow, fragrant flowers.

Two species in particular, *Acacia baileyana* and *Acacia farnesiana*, are suitable for bonsai training as they do not grow as big as the other species. In Europe both species are most commonly found along the French Riviera.

Acacia baileyana must be kept cool over winter whereas *A. farnesiana* is able to adapt to the warmer temperatures found in most houses. Should only be repotted about once every two years.

Albizia julibrissin

Deciduous trees with pinnate leaves and light pink flowers, distributed over a wide area in the tropics and subtropics of the Old and New worlds. It should be cultivated as a cold-house bonsai.

Araucaria heterophylla (excelsa) Araucaria pine	One of the best-known trees from subtropical regions, providing few problems as an indoor bonsai. It can tolerate warm temperatures and does not even object to dryness, although it does not like glaring sunshine.
Ardisia crenata Spear-flower	Very small, evergreen trees and shrubs with off-white flowers and red berries the size of a pea. Makes a delightful bonsai as it retains its berries for several months, provided that it is kept in a very bright spot and overwintered at a temperature of 15–18°C (59–64°F). Spear-flowers tend to produce a complex branch network.
Bambusa multiplex Bamboo	A large number of these tropical, woody grasses are also found in the Mediterranean area. *Bambusa multiplex* is particularly suitable for keeping as an indoor plant. It requires a very bright site (but avoid brilliant sunshine during summer), a lot of water and a winter temperature range of 20–22°C (68–72°F). Bamboo grasses develop their new leaves in the tip of their shoots. Simply nip them out before they unfurl, to keep your bonsai nice and compact.
Bougainvillea glabra Lesser Bougainvillea	A decorative ornamental shrub with very pretty flowers, white, scarlet or lilac in colour. To make the bougainvillea flower each year it will need to undergo a winter dormancy at a low temperature. Transfer the plant to somewhere warm and bright from early spring onwards. Water sparingly in winter and thoroughly in summer. Bougainvilleas will shed their leaves if kept warm over winter (over 18°C, 64°F) or if they are kept too moist.
Bucida spinosa Dwarf Black Olive	A delicate tree from the Caribbean that grows into a bonsai shape almost without any assistance. Keep well-watered and prune the roots lightly each year in late winter. Trim back new shoots only slightly (nip them out).
Bursera simaruba Balsam tree	In its Caribbean homeland the American balsam tree can grow as tall as 15 m (50 ft). Its most striking feature is a red-brown trunk with a layer of bark that looks like see-through paper. The leaves are pinnate and the flowers greenish-yellow. Every part

of the tree is aromatic. As an indoor bonsai *Bursera simaruba* makes few demands; it tolerates warmth and dryness. Cuttings take root very quickly in moist earth.

Small, evergreen, mimosa-like shrubs with pinnate leaves and decorative white or red flowers. They are native to the tropics of America and Asia and are found along the Mediterranean in Europe. As an indoor bonsai they do best in a warm, sunny window site. Keep evenly moist at all times, and give a bit of extra water if temperatures are fairly high.	**Calliandra** Powder Puff
This is a tropical shrub belonging to the waxy trees. It is an evergreen with small leaves and thorns. If kept in a very bright location it will develop fragrant, white-pink flowers and edible dark red fruits. Water moderately and keep warm over winter. Repot in autumn and winter only, pruning the roots only slightly as you do so.	**Carissa macrocarpa** Christ's Thorn; Natal Plum
This species is long known to have been a medicinal plant amont North American Indian tribes. It has a slightly woody trunk, gracefully constructed leaves and small yellow flowers. Even in nature it only grows 50–100 cm (20–40 in) tall. As an indoor bonsai it is able to tolerate somewhat higher temperatures than *Cassia angustifolia*, for example, and other *Cassia* species, many of which are found as pot or tub plants in subtropical parts of the Mediterranean. In our homes they can be cultivated as cold-house bonsai. Place in a cool site.	**Cassia marylandica** Cassia
Most false cypresses are only suitable as outdoor bonsai, but the varieties given here also flourish indoors. They can tolerate fairly high temperatures provided that the foliage is sprayed frequently, but they should never be placed directly above a radiator. The ideal site, however, is a cool, very bright and well-ventilated window. Moderate watering is required throughout the year, the plant being allowed to dry out a little between waterings.	**Chamaecyparis pisifera** 'Plumosa', **Ch. pisifera** 'Nana Aurea' and **Ch. pisifera** 'Squarrosa' False Cypress

Chrysanthemum frutescens
Common Marguerite

The delicate Marguerite shrub comes originally from the Canary Islands. In the wild it grows between 50 and 150 cm (20–60 in) tall. Indoors, too, this species is covered almost all the year round in a large number of marguerite-like flowers.

It makes a very pretty, vigorously growing bonsai. Requires cold-house conditions: a bright site, cool overwintering and moderate watering.

Cinnamomum camphora
Camphor tree

Camphor trees are found in tropical and subtropical parts of Asia. They sometimes grow up to 40 m (130 ft) tall and develop powerful-looking trunks covered with a thick, fissured bark. The shiny ovoid leaves grow thickly and are often too big for the tree once trained as a bonsai, but gradually they will get smaller. Camphor trees like a bright and fairly warm site.

Citrus microcarpa

See *Fortunella hindsii*, p. 48.

Coffea arabica and **C. robusta**
Coffee bush

The tropical coffee bush makes a charming specimen all year round with its shiny, dark-green, evergreen leaves, its white, star-shaped summer flowers and its red winter berries. In summer it needs a semi-shaded site, certainly not by a hot southerly window; in winter it needs to be stood somewhere very bright. During the growing period spray it frequently and immoderately; in winter water sparingly, depending on room temperature, but never allow to dry out. The ideal overwintering temperature range is 16–22°C (61–72°F).

Cotoneaster microphyllus, C. microphyllus cochleatus
Cotoneaster

Both of these cotoneasters are slow-growing evergreens with small leaves, white flowers and red berries. Kept in a cold-house environment, cotoneasters make very attractive indoor bonsai and are ideally suited for training as miniature bonsai.

A miniature shrub from Central America with small, narrow leaves and delicate, crimson flowers. Also good as a miniature bonsai. Never allow the plant to dry out, but keep slightly moist at all times. A sunny, warm site is important.

Cuphea hyssopifolia
Japanese Myrtle

This is well-known to us as a hedging plant which produces a profusion of yellow flowers in spring. It can also do well as an indoor bonsai, if cold-house conditions are imposed: an airy, bright but cool site over winter at a temperature of 8–12°C (46–54°F). As a bonsai *Cytisus* prefers a calcareous soil.

Cytisus racemosus

An evergreen ornamental shrub with shiny green foliage, red shoots and white flower panicles. Very good lighting conditions are essential if the tree is to produce its deep red, edible fruits. Like all myrtle species, *Eugenia* likes a slightly acidic soil, but it can overwinter at a considerably higher temperature than its relatives, around 18–20°C (64–68°F).

Eugenia brasiliensis

Evergreen, decorative shrubs with dark green, leathery leaves, small flowers and black, spherical fruits. Keep warm over winter and moist at all times.

Eurya japonica
Japanese Elderberry

Ficus benjamina, F. buxifolia, F. diversifolia, F. natalensis, F. neriifolia reg., F. pumila minima, F. retusa nitida, F. benjamina 'Starlight' – all small-leaved *Ficus* species are eminently suitable for bonsai training. They are described in more detail on page 44.

Ficus
Fig tree

A small, decorative shrub with thin, delicate branches and lovely crimson flowers between mid-summer and mid-autumn. If kept under cold-house conditions fuchsias retain their leaves. For notes on care, see page 54.

Fuchsia magellanica
'Gracilis'
Fuchsia

This densely growing Caribbean tree has a striking whitish-grey bark and vivid blue flowers, which also appear in the bonsai version if the plant is placed somewhere very bright. Keep it warm over winter. Shaping is best done through pruning as the branches are very hard and not very flexible. Allow the soil to dry out slightly between waterings.

Guaiacum officinale
Lignum Vitae;
Pockwood tree

Hedera helix Ivy	A robust houseplant which tolerates cool and warm conditions equally well. However, it takes quite a time for a reasonably thick trunk to develop to give the plant a more tree-like character.
Hibiscus rosa sinensis Blacking Plant	A small tree from the subtropics known to Europeans as an evergreen pot plant with shiny green leaves and large, funnel-shaped, pinky-red flowers. Overwinter at a temperature of 12–15°C (54–59°F) and give plenty of water during the growing season and flowering period. The Blacking Plant can easily be trained as a bonsai.
Hibiscus tiliaceus Lagoon Hibiscus	This species can be overwintered at very warm temperatures. A very bright location is important for the development of leaves and flowers. Allow to dry out a little before watering. This particular *Hibiscus* species will tolerate hard pruning.
Ilex crenata, Ilex crenata 'Marisii' Holly	Low-growing holly species with small leaves. Bonsai shaping is best carried out through pruning methods rather than wiring, as holly branches are brittle. *Ilex vomitoria* develops red berries on the female plant provided the flowers are pollinated beforehand.
Ixora javanica Jungle Geranium	The brilliant red inflorescences on *Ixora* make it one of the most magnificent ornamental shrubs of the tropics. Cultivated as a bonsai it prefers slightly acidic soil. It will grow in less than generous light, but will only flower if stood at a very bright window location with all-year-round temperatures of around 18–22°C (64–72°F).
Leptospermum scoparium Australian Myrtle	An ornamental shrub from New Zealand, this particular myrtle develops needle-shaped, prickle-sharp leaves and small, white, rose-like flowers. Needs a bright but cool site. Keep moist at all times and only prune the roots slightly.
Ligustrum japonicum, L.j. rotundifolium Japanese Privet	The evergreen Japanese Privet is cultivated as an indoor bonsai on account of its rather lovely, shiny green foliage. *Ligustrum lucidum*, in addition, has attractive flowers. Both species prefer to be kept cool over winter, although they are able to adapt to warmer temperatures as well.

Popular in the Western world as a hedging plant, the honeysuckle is an evergreen shrub originating from China. It is well suited to bonsai training. It has a vigorous growth, small leaves and fragrant, white flowers. Likes a bright but cool site.

Lonicera nitida
Honeysuckle

A tropical ornamental shrub from Madagascar with wavy-edged, strongly-veined leaves which can gradually be reduced to 'bonsai size'. Shaping can be done entirely through pruning. Keep warm and stand in a very bright spot over winter.

Nicodemia diversifolia
Indoor Oak

In nature *Nothofagus* is a strikingly tall, evergreen tree. Its vigorous growth and small leaves make it a good candidate for bonsai treatment. Water only moderately but never allow to dry out. Stand somewhere bright and cool.

Nothofagus cunninghamii
Tasmanian Beech

This particular species of pelargonium remains small and is especially recommended for bonsai training. It has heart-shaped or kidney-shaped leaves, grey-green in colour, and flowers ranging from pink to a deep red. Prefers a very bright site and moderate watering – it sheds its leaves if kept too wet. The ideal overwintering temperatures are 16–20°C (61–68°F), but slightly higher ones are tolerable.

Pelargonium rhodanthum
Pelargonium; Geranium

A delicate, evergreen, heather-like shrub with slender, needle-shaped leaves and bundles of white flowers. Makes an attractive indoor bonsai when kept under cold-house conditions. Stand in a very bright, sunny position, water moderately, allow to dry out a little. Use water with minimum calcium content for watering.

Phylica ericoides

Subtropical, summer green and evergreen shrubs with pinnate leaves. *Pistacia terebinthus* also has shiny red fruits in autumn. Native to the Mediterranean, Asia and America, in our climate they should be cultivated as cold-house bonsai. Stand in a very bright spot and water moderately.

Pistacia
Pistachio

Pittosporum tobira	A subtropical, evergreen tree with a dense growth pattern. Has leathery, shiny dark-green leaves and white flowers with a strong smell from mid-spring to early summer. When kept as an indoor bonsai it needs a bright but cool site. In all other respects treat as a myrtle.
Psidium cattleianum Strawberry Guava	A fast-growing, evergreen, tropical shrub with an interestingly flecked bark and white flowers. In South America it is cultivated for its round, edible fruits, crimson in colour; these may also occur on the bonsai version. The strawberry guava can be kept at warm temperatures over winter and needs a bright location.
Pyracantha Pyracantha; Fire-thorn	Species such as *P. angustifolia* and *P. crenata-serrata*, popular in Europe as evergreen hedging, also make decorative indoor bonsai with their small leaves, white spring flowers and red autumnal berries. They prefer to be kept cool in winter. Moderate watering at all times except during the flowering period and when the fruits are ripening, when plenty of water needs to be given.
Quercus suber Cork tree; Cork Oak	A knotty, evergreen tree from the Mediterranean, recommended for bonsai training. Cork trees require cold-house conditions, moderate watering and repotting only about every two or three years. Prune roots only slightly. If collecting your own specimens, choose young plants only as older ones will not tolerate hard pruning.
Raphiolepsis indica Indian Hawthorn	A decorative, slow-growing ornamental shrub that remains low in height. Has leathery leaves and white-pink flowers and later on blue-black fruits. Shaping should be achieved through pruning only as its very brittle branches are difficult to wire. Cold-house conditions are ideal for this subtropical shrub, although it is also able to adapt to warmer temperatures.

This evergreen, aromatic herb can also be cultivated as an indoor bonsai. Choose a plant that already has a slightly woody stem. Wild Rosemary has needle-shaped, green leaves and small whitish-blue or mauve flowers in spring. Is a vigorous grower if stood at a very bright southerly window. Cold-house conditions are required.

Rosmarinus officinalis
Wild Rosemary

A deciduous conifer that makes a decorative indoor bonsai. Prefers to be kept cool and dry over winter during which time it sheds its foliage. From the moment new shoots start to grow in the spring this plant requires a very bright, well-ventilated site and a large amount of water.

Taxodium distichum
Deciduous Cypress;
Black Cypress

An evergreen shrub with elongated, leathery leaves and strong-smelling, white flowers in terminal and axillary racemes. A pretty indoor bonsai that develops well under cold-house conditions.

Trachelospermum jasminoides
Chinese Jasmine

A tropical, evergreen shrub with slender branches and decorative, fuchsia-like flowers, white in colour. Train as an indoor bonsai when the plant is still young. Keep warm over winter, 18–22°C (64–72°F). Spray frequently, as this tree likes a high humidity level, and give plenty of water during its long flowering period.

Wrigthia or **Holarrhena antidysenteria**

Appendix: Useful Addresses

Federation of British Bonsai Societies

Send an S.A.E. with all correspondence.

Secretary, Rivendale, 14 Somerville Road, Sutton Coldfield, West Midlands B73 6JA.

Bedfordshire Bonsai Society, 92 Conniburrow Boulevard, Milton Keynes.

Bonsai Kai, 39 West Square, London SE11 45P.

Bristol B.S., 35 Clevedon Road, Failand, Bristol, Avon.

British Bonsai Association, Flat D, 15 St John's Park, Blackheath, London SE3 7TH.

Cotswold B.S., The Gardens, Catley, Bosbury, Herefordshire HR8 1QF.

Croydon Bonsai Club, 47 Crossways, South Croydon, Surrey CR2 8QJ.

East Midlands Bonsai, Greenwood Gardens, Ollerton Road, Arnold, Notts NG5 8PR.

Humberside Bonsai Club, 43 The Dales, Cottingham, North Numberside HU16 5JS.

Humanby Bonsai Club, 34 Hungate Lane, Humanby, Yorkshire, YO14 0NP.

Kew Kai Bonsai, 7 Crane Park Road, Whitton, Middx TW2 6DF.

Lincoln B.S., 28 Birchwood Avenue, Lincoln LN6 OJB.

Manchester B.S., 160 Cheadle Old Road, Edgerley, Stockport, Cheshire.

Middlesex B.S., 124 Braemar Avenue Neasden, London NW10 0DP.

Midland B.S., 46 Hodge Hill Common, Birmingham, BS36 8AG.

Milton Keynes Bonsai Society, 20 Station Terrace, Great Linford, Milton Keynes.

National B.S., 24 Bidston Road, Liverpool L4 7XJ.

Norfolk Bonsai Society, 7 Broadland Close, Worlingham, Beccles, Suffolk NR34 7AT.

Northern Ireland Bonsai Society, 6 Marina Park, Belfast BT5 6BA.

Scottish B.A., 22 Buccleugh Street, Edinburgh, Scotland EH8 9IL.

Solent B.S., 7 Wakefield Avenue, Fareham, Hants, PO16 7RJ.

Southend Bonsai Society, 45 Brunswick Road, Southend-on-Sea, Essex SS1 2UH.

Sussex B.C., 13 South Way, Burgess Hill, Sussex RH15 9SS.

Waltham Forest, 66 Selwyn Avenue, Highams Park, London E4 9LR.

Yorkshire B.A., 38 Green Lane, Cookridge, Leeds, W. Yorks LS16 7LP.

Main UK Bonsai Dealers

Bonsai Shop, Culver Nurseries Castlegate Road, Enfield, Herts.

Bourne Bridge Nurseries, Oak Hill Road, Stapleford Abbotts, Romford, Essex.

Bromage and Young, St Mary's Gardens, Worplesdon, Surrey GU3 3RS.

Glenbrook Nursery, Stone Edge Batch, Twickenham, Clevedon BS21 6SE.
Greenwood Gardens, Ollerton Road, Arnold, Notts.
Dawn and Peter Chan, Herons Bonsai Ltd, Wire Mill Lane, New Chapel,
Nr Lingfield, Surrey RH7 6HJ.
Middle Earth Bonsai, 249 Lytham Road, Southport, Merseyside.
Meads End Bonsai, Forewood Lane, Crowhurst, Sussex TN33 9AB.
Tokonoma Bonsai, 14 London Road, Shenley, Radlett, Herts.
Potters Garden Bonsai, The Boat House, Potters Lane, Samlesbury, Preston.
Price and Adams, Cherry Trees, 22 Burnt Hill Road, Wrecclesham, Surrey.
Adreanne Weller, St Mary's Garden, Worplesdon, Surrey.

International Contacts

Australia
Mr Lindsay Bebb
8 Fegen Drive, Moorooka, QLD
4105 Australia

J. Farman
Victoria Bonsai Association,
14 Sussex Street,
Brighton 3186,
Victoria, Australia

Mr Frank Hocking
Bonsai in Australia,
14 Newhall Avenue, Moonie Ponds
3039 Australia

Mr Jim Scott
National Bonsai Association
c/o 22 Burraga Avenue, Terrey
Hills, N.S.W. 2084
Australia

Austria
Osterreichischer B C
Zaunmullerstrasse 1, A–4020, Linz,
Austria

Belgium
BBF–FBB Fazantenlaan 31
1900 Overijse
Belgium

Denmark
Dansk B Selskab
Sobredden 22 2820, Gentofte,
Denmark

E. Germany
Heidrun Hunger
Cothnerstr 9, 7022 Leipzig

European Bonsai Association
G.M. De Beule
European Bonsai Association
Heliotropen laan 3,
1030 Brussel, Belgium

Finland
Matti Makinen
Kukkakauppojen Tukky Oy
Valuraudantie 17, SF–00700,
Helsinki

France
French Bonsai Federation
Alle de Duras, St. Benait la Foret,
37500 Chinon

Club Parisienne Du Bonsai
29 Rue Du Roi De Sicilie, 75004,
Paris, France

Greece
Nicolas Rountis
Roynth, Kifissiasn Ave 105A
(Erychros Stavros), Athens

Hungary
Tamas Biro
Dipl. Ing. of Hort., 1126 Budapest,
Margarata Str. 17

India
Indian Bonsai Society,
Mrs L. Jhaveri
105 Samundra Mahal, Dr Annie
Besant Road, Worli, Bombay,
India

Ireland
Irish Bonsai Society
18 Strand Road, Dublin 4

Italy
Bonsai Clubs D'Italia
Str. Mongreno, 341 10132 Torino,
Italy

G. Bruno
Assoc. Italiana Bonsai,
2 50136 Firenze,
Italy

Japan
Mr Y. Nagase
Kawaguchi Bonsai Association
2–1–1 Aoki, Kawaguchi City,
Saitama-Pref. Japan

Nippon Bonsai Association
3–42 Ueno-Koen, Daito-ku,
Tokio, Japan

Luxembourg
Bonsai Club Luxembourg
195 Route de Beggen
L–1221 Beggen

Norway
Karli Ericsen
Asbjornsensgarten 35a, 7000
Trondheim

Portugal
Sr. D. Fausto
Otros Grupos en la Peninsula
Hidalgo de Nascimento, Travesa
dos Moinhos, 20–3

South Africa
Shibui Bonsai Kai
P.O. Box 81084, Parkhurst, 2120

Spain
Assoc. Espanola De Bonsai
Paseo de la Pechina 15. Valencia –8

Sweden
Margit Kaberger
Kornbodsgatin 27, S–72481
Vasteras

Switzerland
Scheizer Bonsai Liebhaberclub
Capuzinerweg 8,
CH–6006 Luzern

U.S.A.
John Y. Naka
Bonsai Institute of California
PO BOX 78211, Los Angeles,
CA 90016–1211

Bill M., Valavanis
412 Pinnacle Road,
Rochester, NY 14623

Bonsai West
213 Washington Street
Brookline
Mass. 02146, U.S.A.

W. Germany
B C Verein Europaischer M
Postfach 106209 6900, Heidelburg,

Bonsai-Centrum Heidelberg
P. Lesniewicz
Manneheim Straat 401,
6900 Heidelburg

Bonsai Museum
Munnheim Strasse 401
6900 Heidelberg

Olea europaea, approximately 75 years old and 68 cm (27 in) high. From the collection of Guido Degl'Innocenti, Italy.

Sources of Starter Material

Hewett and Stewart, 91 Epsom Road, Morden, Surrey (mail order only).
Mount Pleasant Trees, Rockhampton, Berkeley, Gloucs.
Hilliers and Sons, Winchester, Hants SO22 5DN.

Index of Plant Names

Page numbers in *italics* refer to illustrations or diagrams.

General Index

Page numbers in *italics* refer to illustrations or diagrams.